Cuddly Tedd

15 Teddy Bear Patterns

Martini Nel

δελος

Cape Town

To
Adriaan and Martinette

A special word of thanks to my husband, Adri, for his patience
and understanding and for drawing the patterns. Many thanks
also to Dalene Müller, Etienne van Duyker and Trudé Botma
for their assistance.

© 1992 Delos
33 Church Street, Cape Town

Also available in Afrikaans as *Troetelbere*

Photography by Peter Bouman and Anton de Beer (p. 15)
Illustrations by Adri Nel
Styling by Etienne van Duyker
Typography and cover design by Etienne van Duyker
Translated into English by Ethné Clarke
Typeset in 10 on 11 pt New Caledonian Medium by
Martingraphix, Cape Town
Printed and bound by ABC Press, Cape Town
First edition, first impression 1992

ISBN 1-86826-238-3

Contents

Introduction

Teddy bears are amongst the most popular toys in the world. Not only toddlers love these endearing toys; even older children, teenagers and adults adore them. In fact, few people can resist the temptation of touching a soft, woolly teddy bear in passing – just watch next time you visit a toy shop.

One can hardly imagine a time in our history when teddy bears did not exist. They originated almost simultaneously in two places in the world. In Germany Margarete Steiff, who was handicapped, made felt toys such as elephants and other animals. The demand for them was so great that she eventually opened a factory.

In 1903 the Steiff brothers exhibited a soft, woolly bear at the Leipzig Show. It caught the eye of a visiting American, who immediately placed an order for three thousand bears. Soon another order followed – and after that the making and selling of teddy bears caught on in a big way.

Another version of the story is that teddy bears owe their origin to Theodore Roosevelt, president of the United States of America from 1901 to 1909. The story goes that during a hunting trip on 10 November 1902 in the state of Mississippi he encountered a baby bear, which he refused to shoot. The following day the incident was reported in the Washington Post. The newspaper's cartoonist, Clifford Berryman, drew the president standing with his back to a bear and the butt of his rifle resting on the ground. This cartoon attracted much attention and the public began to associate Roosevelt with bears. After that, small bears regularly appeared in Berryman's cartoons.

Morris Michtom, founder of The Ideal Toy Corporation in New York, wrote a letter to the president requesting permission to call the toy bears made by his wife, Rose, after him. (The abbreviated form of Theodore is Teddy.) The president gave his permission, hence the name 'teddy bear'. After that, teddy bears regularly featured at Republican conventions and meetings attended by President Roosevelt, and they soon became popular among children.

However, how and where teddy bears originated is less important than the fact that they are wonderful toys. For many years they have brought joy to thousands of people. They are also popular as mascots, e.g. for sports teams.

Teddy bears are convenient toys to take along, be it on holiday or to hospital – they make themselves at home anywhere! Since they feature in countless books and stories, they are very much part of children's lives at some stage or other.

Teddy bears are not exclusively for children; many teenagers and adults enjoy owning or collecting them. I know of a student who asked his mother to make him a large, cuddly teddy bear to take to university with him.

Make one today for a special person in your life. For Valentine's Day, you could make a red or snow-white bear with a heart or a short message embroidered or appliquéd on his tummy. When you make a teddy bear as a gift, it's a good idea to present him along with a 'birth certificate' inscribed with his name and 'date of birth'.

In this book there are quick and easy patterns for making teddy bears for yourself, your children or grandchildren, or a school or church fête. Begin with a simple teddy bear and progress to a jointed teddy with movable head, arms and legs.

Note that each teddy bear's facial expression is bound to be different, even if you use the same pattern – the photographs serve as a guideline only. Expressions are not necessarily indicated on the patterns.

Usually, when people ask me to teach them to make a teddy bear, they can't believe that it's not necessary to attend a series of classes first – one morning will suffice. It's fun to see a teddy bear taking shape in a jiffy, and to hear about the excitement and pleasure teddy bears bring to the hearts of children and adults.

Materials

Fabric

The artificial fur which is used to make teddy bears is sold locally as 'fun fur' and is therefore referred to by this term throughout the book. It's not necessary to buy fun fur if you want to make a teddy bear immediately. Use any fabric available. You can make one to match the colour scheme of your bedroom – or of the bedroom of the lucky recipient of your gift. If you do not have sufficient fabric for the pattern, you can join small pieces and make a patchwork teddy bear. Just use a little imagination!

However, the kind of fabric a teddy bear is made of will determine the appearance of the end product. If you use fun fur with a long pile (fibres), your teddy bear will be much softer and cuddlier than one with a short pile.

Some inexpensive fun furs have a long pile but are not densely woven, which affects the appearance of the end product. Thickly woven fun fur is a little more difficult to work with than the thinly woven kind but the end result will more than compensate for the time you spend on it.

Cotton and towelling fabrics are very easy to work with, as well as being inexpensive and easily obtainable.

Fun fur

Fun fur is an ideal fabric for making teddy bears. The thicker the fur, the softer and woollier the teddy bear will look. Fun fur is usually available in 150 cm widths and for this reason only the required length is mentioned in the list of materials for each teddy bear.

Because fun fur is generally made of polyester, it is washable.

Fun fur made of wool or mohair can also be used.

Cotton

Ordinary cotton fabric is also suitable for making a teddy, especially if you want it to match a particular colour scheme. One could make a teddy bear of the same fabric as the curtains or accessories of a room.

Unbleached calico is another suitable fabric – it looks particularly attractive on a candlewick quilt – while denim is a good choice for teenagers.

Towelling

Towelling is particularly suitable if you make a teddy bear for a toddler, who will no doubt soon become very attached to it and refuse to give it up to be washed. Towelling teddy bears can be washed often and dried very quickly in a tumble dryer – before the toddler has time to miss his little companion.

Leather

The paws and paw pads of a teddy bear are usually made of either artificial or genuine leather. Only small pieces are needed. A teddy bear made entirely of suede will be really special.

Felt

Felt is also suitable for paws, paw pads and the inside of the ears. A large variety of colours is available. Today, most kinds are washable but it is advisable first to wash the felt before use, since some kinds shrink. Eyes and noses can also be made of felt.

Ready-made eyes and noses

A large variety of plastic eyes and noses is available. Most have a lock washer that is pressed into the back. The washer cannot be removed without the eye being broken, making it completely childproof.

Glass eyes look more natural but they are scarce and not as safe as the plastic ones.

Stuffing

Various kinds of stuffing can be used for making teddy bears. I prefer polyester stuffing since it is easily obtainable, completely washable and soft – it makes a very cuddly teddy bear.

Foam rubber, which is fully washable, is another suitable medium. Because it is rather messy to work with, however, foam rubber is not an ideal stuffing.

If available, sheep wool makes good stuffing. Remnants of fun fur can be cut into small pieces to serve as a stuffing. In earlier times fine wood shavings, normally used for packing fruit, were used for stuffing teddy bears but this is not recommended.

Thread and yarn

Embroidery or knitting yarn is used to embroider noses and mouths. Follow the instructions in Figs. 6a-6i.

Teddy bears are sewn up with strong, matching thread. Always use a double thread and make sure your stitches are sturdy so that buttons, ears, noses, etc, cannot come off easily and be swallowed by young children.

Always use the strongest thread available to sew up your teddy bear. When the head and body are made separately, the head must be sewn at least two or three times around the neck to prevent it from coming apart. Quilting thread, which is very strong, is ideal for this purpose.

'Voice'

Children love teddy bears that can make sounds. A 'voice' (a 'squeaker' or 'growler') usually comes in a cylindrical container. Sew the cylinder up in a piece of fabric and sew the fabric onto the inside of the back. Stuff the teddy bear firmly and sew up as usual.

General instructions

Patterns

Tracing and cutting out

Trace the patterns onto paper or thin cardboard. Cut along the lines. Mark each pattern exactly as shown on the original pattern in the book.

Place the pattern on the wrong (smooth) side of the fabric (the pile or fibres of the fun fur must run from top to bottom, except in the case of the ears, where the pile must run from the bottom upwards). Trace the pattern onto the fabric with a pencil and cut it out.

When two pattern pieces are placed together and their sizes differ slightly (e.g. at the armholes or necklines), stretch one piece a little while easing in the other until they fit neatly. When a pattern piece (e.g. the left or right front) indicates that you must cut 1 + 1 (or 2 + 2), this means that you will have a left piece and a right piece or a mirror image, for instance a left foot and a right foot. Make sure you sew them on correctly!

Enlarging or reducing

Since the space on a page is limited, I could only insert those patterns that fit onto a page. Don't let that put you off. Use a photocopying machine to enlarge or reduce patterns to the desired size. Use the photographs in the book as a guide to see what the teddy bears look like after the patterns have been enlarged.

At some stage or other, most children crave a giant teddy bear. Use any of the usual patterns and enlarge them a few times to the desired size. Do remember, however, to adjust the eyes and nose to the size of the teddy bear. Alternatively, reduce a pattern and make a baby teddy bear for a bigger teddy bear.

Seams

The pieces of all the patterns are stitched with a 6 mm wide seam allowance. Use your machine's presser foot as a guide for the width of the seam allowance. Some machines have a 7 mm wide presser foot, but this should not make too much difference to the seam allowance.

If necessary, fit the pattern pieces together more tightly or loosely before stitching. It is advisable first to pin all the pieces with right sides facing and then to baste them firmly. Turn the pieces right side out to check whether you have basted them together correctly, then turn them to the wrong side again and stitch.

Note: In the instructions for making the different teddy bears I do not repeat all the steps each time. For example, instead of saying pin, baste and stitch each time, I merely say stitch.

When pinning two pieces of fun fur together with the right sides facing, fold the fibres to the inside. This will prevent too many fibres from being stitched into the seam allowance, causing the seam to be too visible. If some fibres are caught in the seam allowance, however, pull them out with a thick needle afterwards.

When assembling a teddy bear, it is advisable to sew the stuffed head to the body first, then the arms and finally the legs. After joining all the parts, stuff and sew up the arms and legs. Finally, stuff and sew up the body.

How to make the joints

To make a teddy bear with a movable head, arms and legs, you will need joints consisting of a cotter pin, two washers and two round hardboard discs with a diameter of about 5 cm (Fig. 1). The discs, with a thickness of about 6 mm, can also be cut from a dowel rod with a diameter of about 5 cm. Alternatively, cut them from thick, sturdy cardboard and glue the discs together in twos or threes. This will mean that your teddy bear will not be washable, since water will soften the cardboard. The outside can be wiped clean with a damp cloth, however.

Drill or make a hole in the centre of each disc for the cotter pin to pass through.

Place the pattern pieces for the back and the front of each arm or leg together with the right sides facing and stitch right around, leaving an opening at the top. Turn right side out.

Decide where the arm or the leg is to be attached to the body. Make a mark on the wrong side (inside) of the arm or leg and the body. Pass the cotter pin through a washer and a disc. Make a hole in the fabric where you made the mark and push the pin through the fabric – the washer and disc cannot be pulled through. Make sure that the joint is placed in such a way that the seam allowance is wide enough to sew up the remainder of the seam.

Make a hole through the mark inside the body. Pass the cotter pin from the arm or leg through the hole and then through the second disc and washer. Bend the ends of the pin to secure the joint (Fig. 2).

Place the head in position when it is complete, in other words the eyes must already be in position. Stuff the head firmly. Baste along the seam allowance at the neckline using a double thread. Pass the cotter pin first through a washer and then through a disc. Place the disc in the head so that the ends of the cotter pin point to the outside (Fig. 3a). Pull the thread taut and end off firmly (Fig. 3b).

Baste along the seam allowance at the neckline of the body. Pull the threads taut and end off firmly. Pass the ends of the cotter pin through the gathered neck and then through a washer and a disc. Bend the ends of the pin to secure the joint (Fig. 4).

To make the joints move easily and to prevent the discs from damaging the fabric, a piece of leather or felt can be cut and threaded over the cotter pin between the disc and the fun fur. This is not essential, however.

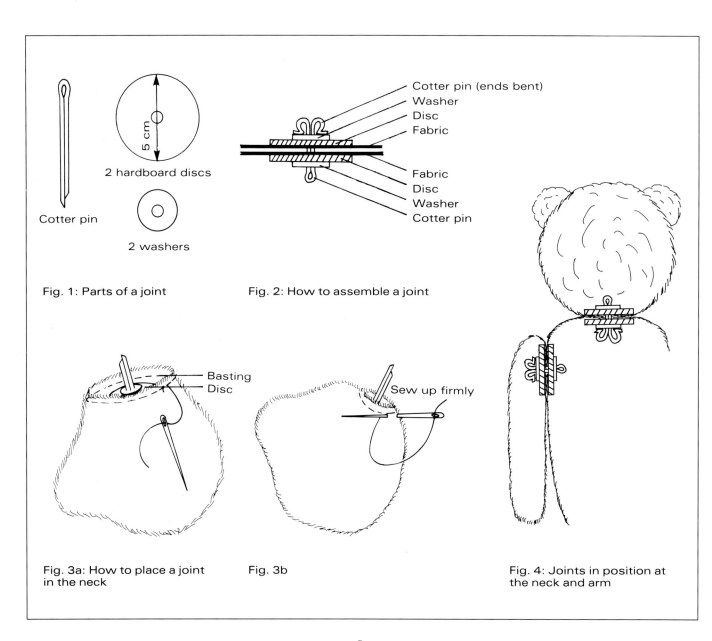

Cotter pin

5 cm

2 hardboard discs

2 washers

Fig. 1: Parts of a joint

Cotter pin (ends bent)
Washer
Disc
Fabric
Fabric
Disc
Washer
Cotter pin

Fig. 2: How to assemble a joint

Basting
Disc

Fig. 3a: How to place a joint in the neck

Sew up firmly

Fig. 3b

Fig. 4: Joints in position at the neck and arm

Eyes

The position of the eyes is not indicated on all the patterns, to allow you to place them where you wish and because the shape of your teddy bear's head may differ from the one I made.

Complete the head and stuff it temporarily. Place the eyes at the front of the head to determine the position and make a mark or insert a pin where the eyes have to come. (A teddy bear's eyes are usually quite far apart. They should not be placed too high – they are usually closer to the muzzle than to the ears.) Remove the stuffing and place the eyes in position.

If plastic eyes are unobtainable or if you wish to make the eyes yourself, felt will serve the purpose. For each eye cut a small circle from black felt, a slightly larger circle from brown felt and a large circle from white felt. Sew the black circle to one side of the brown circle with small stitches. Sew these two circles onto the white circle (Fig. 5a). Use matching thread each time.

Use white embroidery or knitting yarn to embroider white stripes on each eye as shown in Fig. 5b. Decide where you wish to place the eyes and mark the position, making sure that both eyes look in the same direction, for example, to the left. Sew small hemming stitches right around the eyes, leaving a small opening through which to stuff the eyes with small pieces of stuffing. Use a large needle or toothpick to push the stuffing in (Fig. 5c). Sew up the opening.

Nose

Black knitting or six-strand black embroidery yarn is normally used for the nose. Trim off most of the long fibres at the spot where the nose is to be embroidered.

Make a knot in the yarn. Insert the needle exactly in the centre of the nose position and bring it out below the centre. Insert the needle at the top to the left of the knot and out again in the centre (Fig. 6a). Then insert the needle at the top to the right of the knot and out through the centre to form a V (Fig. 6b). Fill the whole area with stitches (Fig. 6c). Sew a few stitches across the top (Fig. 6d) and bring the needle out slightly below the V (the tip of the nose) (Fig. 6e) and then take it back to the tip of the nose (Fig. 6f).

Mouth

Sew a stitch diagonally downwards for the first part of the mouth (Fig. 6g) and then a small stitch diagonally upwards (Fig. 6h). Complete the other side in the same manner as shown in Fig. 6i. End off with a few stitches under the nose so that the stitches are not too noticable, and cut the thread.

Paw pads

When making the paw pads, keep the natural shape of a paw in mind. Fold the pad in half lengthwise and mark the centre – that is, centre back and centre front. With right sides facing, pin the centre back of the pad onto the centre back of the leg, and the centre front of the pad onto the centre front of the leg. If the pad is too large, make the seam allowance a little wider, and vice versa. Alternatively, gather the leg slightly to fit the pad. Stitch the pad on or sew it on by hand.

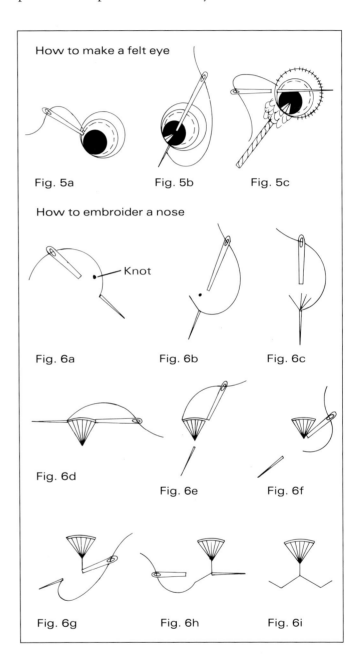

How to make a felt eye

Fig. 5a   Fig. 5b   Fig. 5c

How to embroider a nose

Fig. 6a   Fig. 6b   Fig. 6c

Fig. 6d   Fig. 6e   Fig. 6f

Fig. 6g   Fig. 6h   Fig. 6i

Teddy bears

Panda

Photograph on p. 11 and pattern on pp. 26-29

Materials

30 cm black fun fur
30 cm white fun fur
Remnants of black felt
2 eyes, 20 mm in diameter
Black embroidery yarn
Matching thread
Polyester stuffing

Instructions

Cut the nose from the black felt and all the other pattern pieces from the black and white fun fur as indicated on each piece.

Place the ears together in pairs with right sides facing and stitch along the outer edge. Turn right side out.

Place the front pieces of the head together with right sides facing and stitch the top centre front seam. Fold the muzzle in half with right sides facing and stitch the two short seams. Stitch the muzzle and the curve of the front together, right sides facing. Place the centre front seams of the front together with right sides facing and stitch up to the neckline.

Place the two back pieces of the head together with right sides facing and stitch the top 3 cm of the centre back seam. Place the ears in position on the front and stitch.

Place the front and the back of the head together with right sides facing and fold the ears to the inside. Stitch from the neckline right around and back to the neckline. Turn right side out.

Place the two front pieces of the body together with right sides facing and stitch the centre front seam. Place the chest and the front of the body together with right sides facing and stitch from A to B. Place the inner arms on either side of the chest with the right sides facing and stitch. Place the front pieces of the body and the legs (inner legs) together with the right sides facing and stitch. Place the two back pieces of the body together with the right sides facing and stitch the bottom 12 cm of the centre back seam. Place the back pieces of the arms and legs (i.e. the outer arms and legs) and the back of the body together with the right sides facing and stitch.

Place the front and the back of the body together with right sides facing and stitch on either side of the neckline up to the openings for the paw pads. Stitch the inner leg seams. Do not turn the body and the limbs right side out.

Place the paw pads in the openings of the legs with the right sides facing and stitch together.

Place the body and the head together with right sides facing (the head is now inside the body) and stitch firmly at the neckline. Turn right side out.

Trim the fur slightly where the two black patches around the eyes have to come. Paste the patches in position with clear Bostik and sew neatly to the face around the edges. (If preferred, a small seam allowance can be folded in before you glue the patches in position.) Place the eyes and the nose in position. Fold in a seam allowance of 5 mm around the nose and baste with small stitches. Gather slightly. Lightly stuff the nose and sew it to the muzzle. Remove the basting. Embroider the mouth, using the black embroidery yarn.

Stuff the panda and sew it up at the back.

Place the two pieces of the tail together with the right sides facing and stitch along the outer edge. Turn right side out. Turn in the seam allowance at the bottom edge and baste. Stuff the tail and sew it to the back.

Panda and polar bear.

Polar bear

Photograph on pp. 11, 13 and 19 and pattern on pp. 30-33

Materials

35 cm fun fur
2 eyes, 15 mm in diameter
Matching thread
Black knitting yarn
Polyester stuffing

Instructions

Cut the pattern pieces from the fun fur.

Place the ears together in pairs with the right sides facing and stitch along the outer edge. Turn right side out.

Stitch the darts in the two front pieces of the head. Place the two pieces together with right sides facing and stitch the top centre front seam.

Place the muzzle and the curve of the front together with the right sides facing and the A's corresponding and stitch. Fold the muzzle and the front so that the centre front seams correspond and stitch up to the neckline. Place the ears in position on the front of the head and stitch.

Stitch the two back pieces of the head together, right sides facing, along the bottom 6 cm of the centre back seam. Place the back and the front of the head together with the right sides facing and the ears folded to the inside. Stitch from the neckline right around and back to the neckline. Turn right side out.

Place the back pieces of the body together with right sides facing and stitch the bottom 6 cm of the centre back seam. Place the back of the body and the back of the legs together with the right sides facing. Make small gathers in the legs to make them fit between B and C and stitch.

Stitch the darts in the front of the body at the arms and the legs. Place the two pieces of the front together with right sides facing and stitch the centre front seam.

Place the front and the back of the body together with the right sides facing. Stitch on either side of the neckline right around the arms up to the openings for the paw pads. Stitch the inner leg seams.

With right sides facing, stitch the paw pads into the openings in the legs. Do not turn the body and limbs right side out.

Fold in the seam allowance along the neckline of the head and the body and baste with small stitches. Gather lightly, if necessary. Place the head and body together (the head is now inside the body) with right sides and the centre front seams facing and stitch. Turn right side out.

Stuff the muzzle. Sew long crisscross stitches from side to side through the seam allowance behind the stuffed muzzle to prevent the stuffing from protruding from the muzzle into the head. Place the eyes in position. Embroider the nose and the mouth, using the black knitting yarn.

Stuff the whole bear and sew up at the back.

Tiny Tot

Photograph on p. 13 and pattern on pp. 42-43

Materials

35 cm × 75 cm fun fur
2 eyes, 10 mm in diameter
Black embroidery yarn
Matching thread
Ribbon
Polyester stuffing

Instructions

Cut out the pattern pieces and a circle with a diameter of 6 cm from the fun fur.

Place the front and the back of the body together with the right sides facing. Stitch right around, leaving an opening of about 10 cm in one side. Turn right side out.

Work a row of stitches across the base of the ears to distinguish them from the rest of the face.

Baste right around the circle about 5 mm from the edge. Gather until a small ball is formed. Stuff lightly. Pull the thread a little tighter and end off. Sew the muzzle to the head.

Place the eyes in position. Embroider the rest of the face with the black embroidery yarn.

Stuff the bear. Turn in the seam allowance at the opening and sew up the side seam with small stitches. Tie the ribbon around the bear's neck and make a bow.

A happy Christmas scene with a polar bear, two honey bears and Tiny Tot in bright-yellow fun fur.

Ginger bear

Photograph on p. 15 and pattern on pp. 34-37

Materials

40 cm dark-brown fun fur
1 plastic nose
2 eyes, 15 mm in diameter
Polyester stuffing
Matching thread
Black embroidery or knitting yarn

Instructions

Cut the pattern pieces from the fun fur.

Place the ears together in pairs with the right sides facing and stitch along the outer edge. Turn right side out. Stitch the ears in position onto the sides of the head.

Place the gusset between the two sides of the head with right sides facing and A's and B's corresponding. Stitch on both sides.

Place the muzzle and the curve of the front of the head together with right sides facing and C's corresponding, and stitch. Fold the front and the muzzle with the right sides together so that the centre front seams correspond. Stitch together up to the neckline.

Place the two back pieces of the head together with the right sides facing and stitch the centre back seam.

Place the front and the back of the head together with the right sides facing and the ears folded to the inside. Stitch from the neckline right around and back to the neckline. Turn right side out. Baste 5 mm from the neckline and gather slightly so that the head and the body fit at the neck.

Stitch the back of the legs and the back of the body together with the right sides facing and D's and E's corresponding.

Stitch the darts in the front of the body at the arms and legs. Place the top of the feet and the front of the legs together with right sides facing and stitch.

Place the two front pieces of the body together with the right sides facing and stitch the centre front seam. Place the front and the back of the body together with the right sides facing. Stitch on either side of the neckline right around the arms up to the openings for the paw pads. Leave an opening of about 10 cm in one side through which to stuff the bear. Stitch the inner leg seams.

With right sides facing, stitch the paw pads into the openings in the legs. Do not turn the body and the limbs right side out.

Stuff the muzzle. Sew long crisscross stitches from side to side through the seam allowance behind the muzzle to prevent the stuffing from protruding from the muzzle into the head. Place the eyes in position. Embroider the nose and the mouth with the black yarn.

Place the head and the body together with right sides facing (the head is now inside the body) and stitch. If it is difficult to machine stitch, the seam can be sewn by hand, using a strong thread. Use at least two rows of stitches to prevent the head and the body from coming apart. Turn right side out.

Stuff the bear and sew up the side seam.

Mobile

Photograph on p. 15 and pattern on p. 43

Materials

Remnants of felt in different colours
Black embroidery yarn
Polyester stuffing
Matching thread
1,3 m cord
Variety of ribbons for decoration
80 cm red and green ribbon, 10 mm wide
1 curtain ring
Inner ring of embroidery frame, 18 cm in diameter
Bostik

Instructions

Fold the felt in half and pin. Lightly trace the pattern piece onto the felt with a pencil and stitch along the line all the way around. Cut the teddy bear out about 2 mm from the stitching line.

Using scissors with sharp points, make a small incision at the back of the bear. Stuff the bear and sew up the opening neatly. Embroider the eyes, nose and mouth. Repeat with the other three little bears.

Tie a ribbon around each bear's neck or decorate each one differently. Sew small buttons onto the chest or make a little skirt from a bit of ribbon and lace. Use your imagination.

Apply a little Bostik to the inner ring of the embroidery frame and wrap the ribbon around the ring. I placed a green and a red ribbon, each 10 mm wide, side by side and then wrapped them around the ring together.

Cut two pieces of cord, each about 65 cm long. Thread both pieces through the curtain ring and sew each end to the back of one of the bears. Glue or sew the cord to the embroidery frame a short distance from the end. Make sure that all the teddy bears hang at different levels.

Cut four pieces of ribbon, each about 20 cm long, tie small bows and paste them onto each spot where the cord is attached to the embroidery frame.

Tie a piece of ribbon, about 30 cm long, around the cords where they pass through the curtain ring and make a bow.

The ginger bear with a colourful teddy bear mobile.

Sleeping teddy bear

Photograph on p. 17 and pattern on pp. 38-39

Materials

50 cm fun fur
Black embroidery or knitting yarn
Matching thread
Polyester stuffing

Instructions

Cut the pattern pieces out of the fun fur. If preferred, fabric of a contrasting colour can be used for the paw pads and the ears.

Place the two front pieces of the body (i.e. the bottom) together with the right sides facing and stitch the centre front seam. Place the two back pieces (i.e. the top) together with the right sides facing and stitch the centre back seam, leaving an opening of about 10 cm through which to stuff the bear. Place the front and the back together with right sides facing, and stitch on either side of the neckline right around the arms up to the openings for the paw pads. Stitch the inner leg seams. With right sides facing, stitch the paw pads into the openings in the legs. Do not turn right side out.

Place the ears together in pairs with the right sides facing and stitch around the outer edge. Turn in the seam allowance at the bottom edge and sew up the ears.

Place the sides of the head together with the right sides facing and stitch from A to B. Place the gusset between the two sides of the head with the right sides facing and the B's corresponding and stitch from C up to B and back to C. Turn right side out. Place the ears in position and sew on neatly.

With the right sides facing, stitch the head and the body together at the neck. Make sure the bear's face is turned to one side as if he were sleeping on his tummy. Stuff the head and the body firmly. Sew up the opening at the back. Using black embroidery or knitting yarn, embroider the eyes of a sleeping bear (or use two plastic eyes) and also a nose and a mouth on the face.

Honey bear

Photograph on p. 17 and pattern on pp. 40-42

Materials

45 cm fun fur
2 eyes, 10 mm in diameter
Black embroidery or knitting yarn (or ready-made plastic nose)
Matching thread
Ribbon
Polyester stuffing

Instructions

Cut the pattern pieces from the fun fur.

Stitch the darts in the back of the body. Place the two pieces of the back of the body together with the right sides facing and stitch the centre back seam.

Place the two front pieces together with right sides facing and stitch the centre front seam. Place the front and the back of the body together with the right sides facing and stitch from under the one arm right around, leaving an opening of about 10 cm in the side. Turn right side out.

Place the eyes in position. Work a row of stitches across the base of each ear to distinguish the ears from the rest of the face. Stuff the bear. Turn in the seam allowance at the opening and sew up the side seam with small stitches.

Embroider the nose with the black embroidery or knitting yarn, or use a ready-made plastic nose. Tie a pretty ribbon around the bear's neck and make a bow.

Seven-circle bear

Photograph on pp. 17 and 19 and pattern of ear on p. 42

Materials

35 cm fun fur
2 eyes, 10 mm in diameter
Black embroidery yarn
Matching thread
Polyester stuffing

Instructions

Cut out the pattern pieces for the ears and the following seven circles from the fun fur: one with a diameter of 32 cm for the body, one with a diameter of 22 cm for the head, two with a diameter of 16 cm for each of the legs, two with a diameter of 14 cm for each of the arms and one with a diameter of 6 cm for the muzzle. (The circles can easily be drawn using saucers, side plates, cups, etc.)

Baste close to the edge of each circle and gather slightly. Stuff all the circles. Place the eyes in position on the head. Pull the basting of each circle taut and end off firmly.

First place the stuffed circles for the body and the head

A sleeping teddy bear with a small honey bear in the background and two seven-circle bears in different sizes.

together with the gathered edges facing and sew together firmly right around a few times. Sew the arms, legs and muzzle in position.

Place the ears together in pairs with the right sides facing and stitch along the outer edges. Turn right side out. Turn in the seam allowance at the bottom edge and sew up the ears.

Sew the ears in position. Embroider the nose and the mouth with the black embroidery yarn. (If preferred, the eyes can also be embroidered.)

Change the size of the circles if you wish to have a bigger or a smaller teddy bear. This is an ideal pattern for a child to make, since it can be sewn by hand.

Jointed teddy bear

Photograph on p. 19 and pattern on pp. 44-47

Materials

40 cm fun fur
Leather remnants
5 joints (cotter pins with washers and discs)
2 eyes, 20 mm in diameter
1 plastic nose
Black embroidery yarn
Matching thread
Polyester stuffing

Instructions

Cut the paws and paw pads from the leather. Cut all the other pattern pieces from the fun fur.

Place the ears together in pairs with the right sides facing and stitch along the outer edge. Turn right side out. Turn in the seam allowance at the bottom edge and sew up the ears.

Place the two sides of the head together with right sides facing and stitch from A to B. Stitch the darts in the sides. Place the gusset between the two sides, with right sides facing and B's corresponding and stitch together on both sides. Turn right side out.

Place the eyes in position. Place the ears in position on the front of the head and sew them on. Turn in the seam allowance of the neckline and baste with small stitches. Stuff the head firmly. Insert a cotter pin through one of the discs. Place the disc in the head. Pull the basting in slightly so that the disc cannot come out. End off firmly.

Place the two front pieces of the body together with the right sides facing and stitch the centre front seam. Place the two back pieces together with right sides facing and stitch 5 cm at the bottom and 5 cm at the top of the centre back seam. Place the front and the back of the body together with the right sides facing and stitch both sides. Turn in the seam allowance at the neck and baste with small stitches. Gather slightly. Place the other disc inside the body. Place the head and the body together and push the ends of the cotter pin through the second disc. Bend the ends of the pin.

Place the front paws and the inner arms together with the right sides facing and stitch. Place the inner and outer arms together with right sides facing and stitch, leaving an opening between the two dots at the top. Turn right side out.

Place the inner and the outer legs together with the right sides facing and stitch from the bottom edge on the one side right around to the bottom on the other side, leaving an opening between the two dots at the top. Stitch the paw pads into the openings, right sides facing. Turn right side out.

Place the arms in position. Insert a cotter pin through one disc and place the disc inside the body where one arm has to come. Place the other disc against the inside of the inner arm and push the ends of the cotter pin through the disc. Bend the ends of the pin. Repeat with the other arm.

Place the legs in position. Push a cotter pin through one disc and place the disc inside the body where one leg has to come. Place the other disc against the inside of the inner leg and push the ends of the cotter pin through the disc. Bend the ends of the pin. Repeat with the other leg.

Stuff the legs and the arms and sew up the openings. Stuff the body and sew up at the back. Embroider the nose and the mouth with the black embroidery yarn.

Waistcoat

Photograph on p. 19 and pattern on p. 64

Materials

20 cm fabric for the outer layer
20 cm fabric for the inner layer
4 buttons
2 press studs
Matching thread

Instructions

Cut the pattern pieces from the fabric for the outer and inner layers.

Place the two front pieces and the back of the outer layer together with the right sides facing and stitch the side seams. Place the front pieces and the back of the inner layer together with right sides facing and stitch the side seams.

Place the outer and inner layers together with the right sides facing and stitch right around, but leave the shoulder seams open. Turn right side out. (If the opening at the shoulder seams is too small, leave an opening of about 10 cm at the back so that you can turn the garment right side out through the opening. Sew it up afterwards.)

Match the shoulder seams of the front of the outer layer to those of the back and stitch. Turn in the seam allowance of the inner layer and sew up the shoulder seams with small stitches. The waistcoat is now reversible. (I used denim for one layer of my teddy bear's waistcoat, and blue fabric with a white motif for the other layer.) Sew the press studs in position. If you want a reversible waistcoat, sew buttons onto the inside and the outside so that it looks as if the waistcoat fastens with buttons.

A teddy bear's picnic with two jointed teddy bears – one dressed in a pinafore and the other in a waistcoat. Between them is a honey-coloured version of the polar bear and far right a chubby seven-circle bear.

Pinafore

Photograph on p. 19

Materials

17 cm × 70 cm printed fabric for the skirt
10 cm × 10 cm printed fabric for the bib
15 cm × 35 cm white fabric for the apron
90 cm lace
150 cm ribbon, 1 cm wide
Matching thread

Instructions

Zigzag the raw edges of all three pieces of fabric. Turn in a hem of about 1 cm along the two short sides and the bottom long side of both the skirt and the apron and stitch.

Work a row of straight stitches along the top of the skirt as well as the apron. Gather until the edge of the skirt measures about 30 cm and that of the apron about 20 cm. Place the gathered edges of the skirt and the apron together with the centre front corresponding and both right sides facing upwards and stitch.

Stitch the lace onto three sides of the bib. If you wish, cut a slight curve at the two top corners before zigzagging. Place the side without the lace on the gathered edge of the skirt with the centre front corresponding and right sides facing. Stitch. Place a piece of the ribbon of about 70 cm long over the raw edge of the skirt so that the ends extend for the same length on either side (for tying the bow). Stitch the ribbon in position. Sew two pieces of ribbon, each 40 cm long, to either side of the top of the bib and tie a bow at the back. Decorate the skirt with lace and ribbon as desired. The straps of the pinafore do not have to be of ribbon – cut strips of fabric and use these to make the straps.

Koala

Photograph on p. 21 and pattern on pp. 48-51

Materials

50 cm grey fun fur
Remnant of white fun fur
Black felt
2 eyes, 20 mm in diameter
Black embroidery yarn
Matching thread
Polyester stuffing

Instructions

Cut a nose and a mouth from the black felt. Cut the pattern pieces for the ears from the white fun fur and all the other pattern pieces from the grey fun fur.

Place a white ear on a grey ear with right sides facing. Repeat with the other two ears. Stitch together along the outer edge. Turn right side out.

Place the gusset between the two sides of the head and, with right sides facing, stitch together on both sides. With right sides facing, stitch the muzzle and the curve of the front of the head together. Fold the front and the muzzle with the right sides together so that the centre front seams correspond and stitch up to the neckline.

Place the two ears in position on the front of the head and stitch.

Place the two back pieces of the head together with the right sides facing and stitch the top 8 cm of the centre back seam.

Place the back and the front of the head together with the right sides facing and the ears folded inwards. Stitch from the neckline right around and back to the neckline. Turn right side out.

Place the arms together in pairs with the right sides facing and stitch right around, leaving an opening of about 6 cm at the top. Stuff the arms and sew up the openings. Place the legs together in pairs with right sides facing and stitch from the bottom edge right around to the other bottom edge, leaving an opening of about 6 cm in the side.

With right sides facing, stitch the paw pads into the openings in the legs. Turn right side out. Stuff the legs and sew up the openings.

Place the two pieces of the front of the body together with the right sides facing and stitch the centre front seam. Place the two pieces of the back of the body together with the right sides facing and stitch the centre back seam, beginning about 12 cm from the top. Place the front and back of the body together with the right sides facing. Stitch from the neckline right around and back to the neckline. Do not turn the body right side out.

Stuff the muzzle. Sew long crisscross stitches from side to side through the seam allowance behind the muzzle to prevent the stuffing from protruding from the muzzle into the head.

Place the head and the body together with the right sides facing (the head is now inside the body) and stitch along the neckline. Turn right side out.

Place the eyes in position. If the colour of the eyes does not contrast with the colour of the fun fur, cut a piece of white felt slightly larger than the eyes and place it between the eyes and the fun fur.

Fold in a seam allowance of 5 mm around the felt nose and baste with small stitches. Gather a little so that the nose forms a slight bulge. End off firmly. Lightly stuff the nose and sew it in position. Sew the black felt mouth in position as well.

Stuff the koala's head and body. Sew both up at the back. Place the arms and the legs in position and sew them on securely.

Dumpy

Photograph on p. 21 and pattern on pp. 52-55

Materials

30 cm fun fur
Small piece of chintz
2 eyes, 12 mm in diameter
Black embroidery yarn
Matching thread
Polyester stuffing

Instructions

Cut the paw pads and paws from the chintz. Cut all the other pattern pieces from the fun fur.

Place the ears together in pairs with the right sides facing and stitch along the outer edge. Turn right side out. Turn in the seam allowance at the bottom edge and sew up.

Place the two side pieces of the head together with right sides facing and stitch from A to B. Stitch the darts in the gusset and the sides. Place the gusset between the two sides with the right sides facing and stitch both sides. Turn right side out.

Place the eyes in position. Turn in the seam allowance at the neckline and baste. Stuff the head firmly.

Place the two front pieces of the body together with the right sides facing and stitch the centre front seam. Place the two pieces of the back together with the right sides facing and stitch the centre back seam. Place the front and the back of the body together with right sides facing and stitch the side seams. Turn right side out. Stuff the body. Turn in the seam allowance at the neck and baste with small stitches. Gather slightly and end off firmly.

Place the centre front seam of the body and the centre front seam of the head together. Sew the head securely to the body. (Sew at least twice right around to ensure that the seam won't come undone.) Sew the ears in position.

Two koala bears and Dumpy made of olive-green fun fur.

Place the inner and the outer legs together with the right sides facing. Stitch from the bottom edge on one side right around to the bottom on the other side, leaving an opening between the two dots at the top. Stitch the paw pads into the openings in the legs with the right sides facing. Turn right side out. Stuff the legs firmly and sew up the openings at the top.

Stitch the paws and the inner arms together with the right sides facing. Place the inner and the outer arms together with right sides facing, and stitch right around, leaving an opening between the two dots at the top. Turn right side out. Stuff the arms and sew up the openings at the top.

Sew the arms in position. Decide whether you prefer the bear sitting or standing and sew on the legs in the desired position. Embroider the nose and the mouth with the black yarn.

Knitted teddy bears

Photograph on p. 23

These two teddy bears are knitted in the same way; only the number of stitches and rows differ. The measurements of the larger teddy bear are given in brackets. The entire bear is knitted plain, which makes it ideal for children learning to knit. They may need a little help with casting on and off.

Materials

1 × 50 g ball of knitting yarn (or remnants)
Polyester stuffing
Matching thread
One pair 3,25 mm knitting needles

Instructions

Begin with the inner end of the ball of yarn and cast on 12 (18) stitches. Use the outer end to cast on a further 12 (18) stitches with which to knit the two legs. Knit 20 (30) rows in plain.

Now begin with the body. Knit the 24 (36) stitches with the same thread. Knit 20 (36) rows plain. Begin on one side and cast on another 15 (22) stitches. Knit the rest of the row. Cast on the same number of stitches at the other end to form the two arms. Knit 16 (24) rows plain and cast off 18 (26) stitches on either side. Knit 22 (34) rows with the remaining 18 (28) stitches. Cast off. Repeat for the back.

Place the two pieces together. Sew up right around, leaving an opening of about 10 cm in one side. Sew diagonally across the ends at the head to form two ears. Stuff the teddy bear and sew up the side seam. Embroider the face as shown on the photograph.

Hand puppet

Photograph on p. 23 and pattern on pp. 56-57

Materials

30 cm fun fur
2 eyes, 15 mm in diameter
Black embroidery yarn
Matching thread
Polyester stuffing

Instructions

Cut the pattern pieces from the fun fur.

Place the ears together in pairs with the right sides facing and stitch along the outer edge. Turn right side out.

Place the two front pieces of the head together with right sides facing and stitch the top centre front seam. With right sides facing, stitch the muzzle and the curve at the front of the head together. Fold the front and the muzzle with the right sides together so that the centre front seams correspond and stitch up to the neckline. Sew the ears in position at the front of the head.

Place the two back pieces of the head together with the right sides facing and stitch the centre back seam. Place the front and the back of the head together with the right sides facing and the ears folded to the inside. Stitch from the neckline right around and back to the neckline. Turn right side out. Place the eyes in position. Embroider the nose and the mouth.

Turn in the seam allowance at the neck and baste with small stitches. Gather slightly. Stuff the head, leaving a hollow large enough for your finger to fit inside the head.

Place the front and the back of the body together with the right sides facing. Stitch from the bottom edge on the one side right around to the bottom on the other side. Turn right side out. Place the neck of the body in the puppet's head and sew the two together securely. Fold in 1 cm along the bottom edge and stitch.

Cut two squares, each 15 cm × 15 cm. Fold each one in half to form a tube. Stitch the long seam. Stitch the paw pads into one of the openings of each tube with right sides facing. Turn right side out. Stuff the legs and sew up the top ends. Sew the legs to the inside of the front of the body.

Pyjama bag

Photograph on p. 25 and pattern on pp. 58-59

Materials

40 cm fun fur
2 eyes, 20 cm in diameter
Black embroidery yarn
Matching thread
Velcro
Polyester stuffing

Instructions

Cut the pattern pieces from the fun fur.

Place the ears together in pairs with the right sides facing and stitch along the outer edge. Turn right side out.

Place the gusset between the sides of the head with right sides facing and stitch both sides together from A to B. With right sides facing and C's corresponding, stitch the muzzle and the curve of the front together. Fold the front and the muzzle with the right sides together so that the centre front seams correspond and stitch up to the neckline. Place the ears in position on the front and stitch.

Two hand puppets chat with each other while one holds a knitted teddy.

Place the two back pieces of the head together with the right sides facing and stitch the centre back seam. Place the back and the front of the head together with right sides facing and the ears folded to the inside, and stitch from the neckline right around and back to the neckline. Turn right side out.

Stuff the muzzle. Sew long crisscross stitches from side to side through the seam allowance behind the muzzle to prevent the stuffing from protruding into the head. Place the eyes in position. Stuff the head firmly. Turn in the seam allowance at the neck and baste with small stitches. Pull the thread taut and end off firmly.

Place the arms and legs together in pairs with the right sides facing. Stitch right around, leaving an opening where they have to be attached to the body. Turn right side out. Stuff the arms and the legs.

Place the two pieces of the back of the body together with the right sides facing. Stitch 5 cm of the top and the bottom of the centre back seam. Fold the rest of the seam allowance of one side over to the wrong side and sew Velcro onto it. Do not fold in the other seam allowance – finish it off with a row of zigzag stitches if you think it may fray. Stitch the other piece of Velcro onto it. (You can also use a zipp at the back if you prefer.)

Stitch the arms and the legs to the front of the body with the right sides facing. Place the front and the back together with right sides facing and the arms and the legs folded to the inside, and stitch right around.

With right sides facing, sew the head and the body together at the neck. Sew at least twice right around with strong thread.

Embroider the nose and the mouth. Place pyjamas in the bag to give the teddy bear a full, round body.

The pattern can be adjusted so that a hot-water bottle can be placed in the body. Measure the hot-water bottle and compare it with the pattern. Cut the body larger, if necessary. Imagine how cosy a child will feel in bed hugging a warm teddy bear on a cold winter's night!

Patchwork bear

Photograph on p. 25 and pattern on pp. 60-63

Materials

30 cm striped cotton fabric
5 cm × 60 cm light printed cotton fabric
10 cm × 90 cm dark printed cotton fabric
2 eyes, 15 mm in diameter
Black embroidery or knitting yarn
20 cm × 20 cm batting
Polyester stuffing
Matching thread

Instructions

Cut the following strips: two 5 cm × 30 cm strips each from the light printed cotton fabric and three 5 cm × 30 cm strips each from the dark printed cotton fabric.

Cut the ears, paw pads and paws from the dark printed cotton fabric and two ears from the batting. Cut the remaining pattern pieces, except the front, from the striped cotton fabric.

Join the strips as follows: Stitch a dark printed strip onto either side of a light printed strip. Then join another light printed strip and a dark printed strip to the first strips. These five strips now form one wide strip of fabric (Fig. 7a). Cut the long strip into short strips, each 5 cm wide (Fig. 7b). Now join six strips as indicated in Fig. 7c. Trim off the triangular pieces

of fabric (Fig. 7d.) Cut two strips of striped cotton fabric each 20 cm × 35 cm and stitch them onto either side of the patchwork strip (Fig. 7e). Place the pattern piece of the front of the body on the piece of patchwork fabric and cut it out.

Place the ears together in pairs with the right sides facing, pin them to the batting and stitch along the outer edge. Turn right side out.

Place the front pieces of the head together with right sides facing and stitch the top centre front seam.

With right sides facing, stitch the muzzle and the curve of the front of the head together. Fold the front and the muzzle and, with right sides facing, stitch along the centre front seam up to the neckline. Stitch the ears in position as indicated on the pattern piece.

Place the back pieces of the head together with the right sides facing and stitch the top 3 cm of the centre back seam.

Place the front and the back of the head together with the right sides facing and the ears folded to the inside. Stitch from the neckline right around and back to the neckline. Turn right side out. Place the eyes in position.

Stitch the paws and the front of the body together with right sides facing. Place the two pieces of the back of the body together with the right sides facing and stitch the bottom 5 cm of the centre back seam. Stitch the back of the legs to the back of the body with the right sides facing.

Place the front and the back of the body together with the right sides facing. Stitch on either side of the neckline around the arms up to the openings for the paw pads. Stitch the inner leg seams. Do not turn the body and the limbs right side out.

With right sides facing, stitch the paw pads into the openings in the legs.

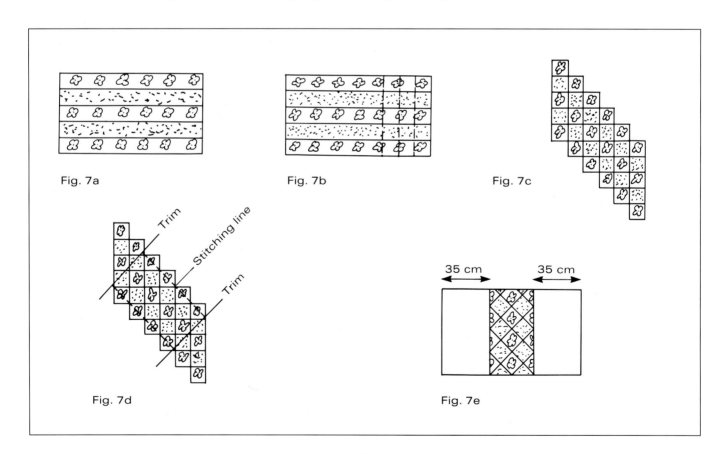

Fig. 7a

Fig. 7b

Fig. 7c

Fig. 7d

Fig. 7e

35 cm   35 cm

Place the head and the body together at the neck with the right sides facing (the head is now inside the body) and stitch. Turn right side out. Embroider the nose and the mouth on the muzzle.

Stuff the teddy bear. Sew up the opening at the back.

The patchwork strips can also be cut narrower and more strips can be joined together. The strips can all be different colours. The whole teddy bear can also be made out of patchwork fabric: first cut enough fabric strips for the whole teddy bear and join them.

The patchwork bear and a cuddly pink pyjama bag with all their little friends.

Patterns

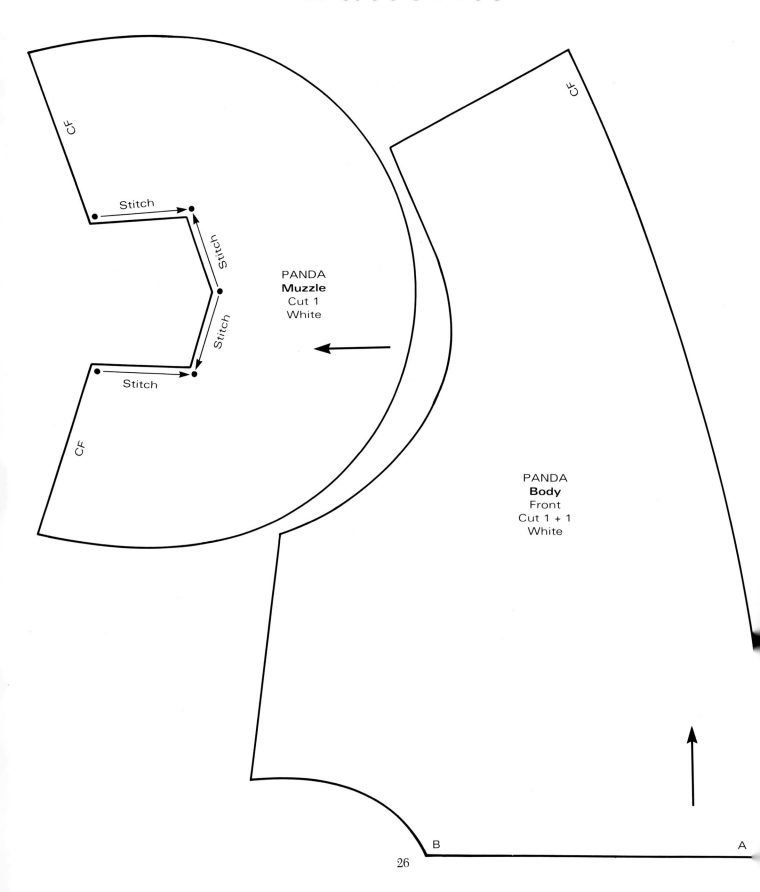

CF

Stitch

Stitch

Stitch

Stitch

Stitch

PANDA
Muzzle
Cut 1
White

CF

CF

PANDA
Body
Front
Cut 1 + 1
White

B

A

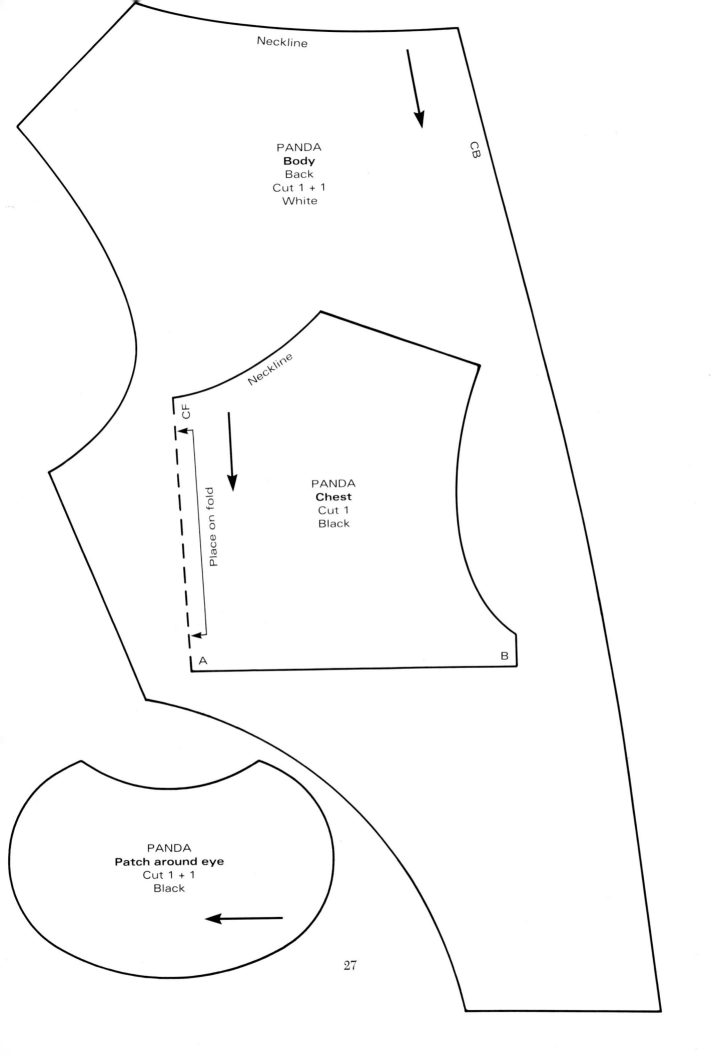

Neckline

PANDA
Body
Back
Cut 1 + 1
White

CB

Neckline

CF

Place on fold

PANDA
Chest
Cut 1
Black

A

B

PANDA
Patch around eye
Cut 1 + 1
Black

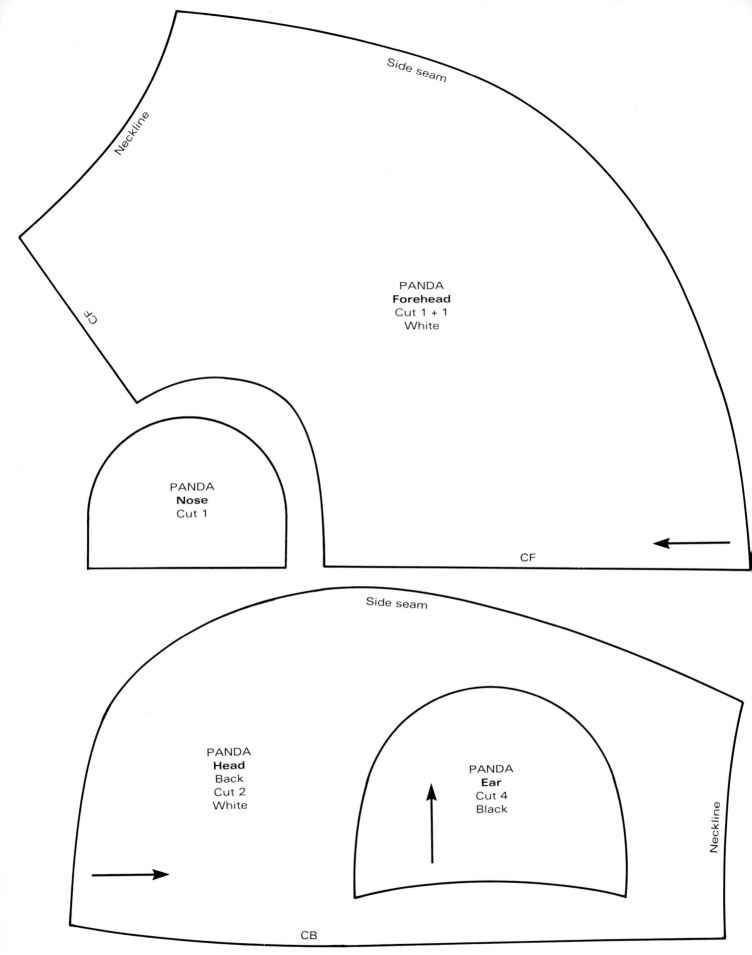

Side seam

Neckline

CF

PANDA
Forehead
Cut 1 + 1
White

PANDA
Nose
Cut 1

CF

Side seam

PANDA
Head
Back
Cut 2
White

PANDA
Ear
Cut 4
Black

Neckline

CB

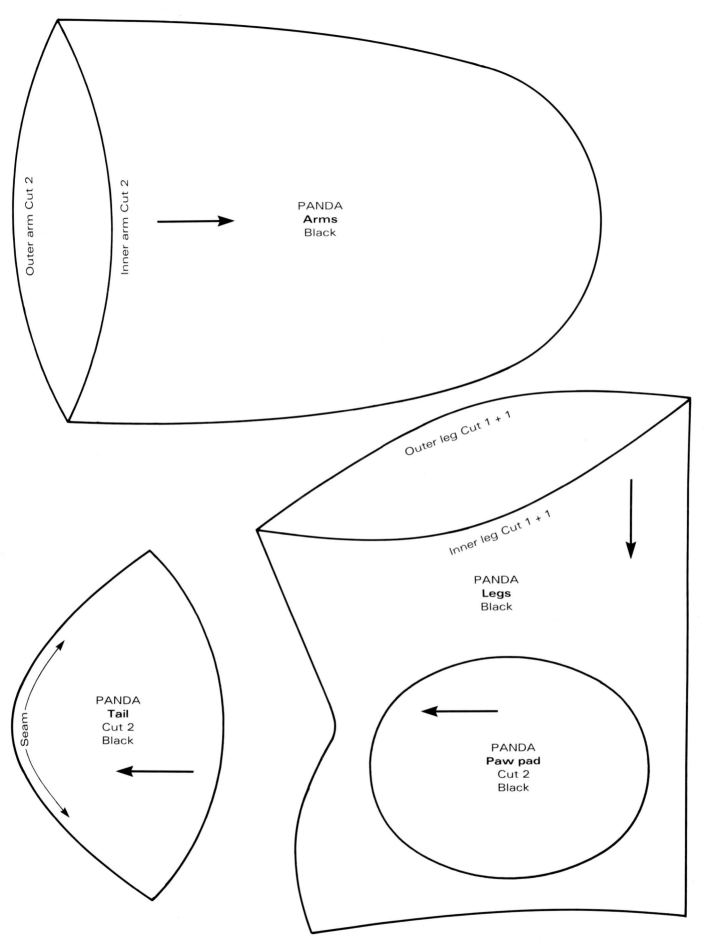

Outer arm Cut 2

Inner arm Cut 2

PANDA
Arms
Black

Outer leg Cut 1 + 1

Inner leg Cut 1 + 1

PANDA
Legs
Black

Seam

PANDA
Tail
Cut 2
Black

PANDA
Paw pad
Cut 2
Black

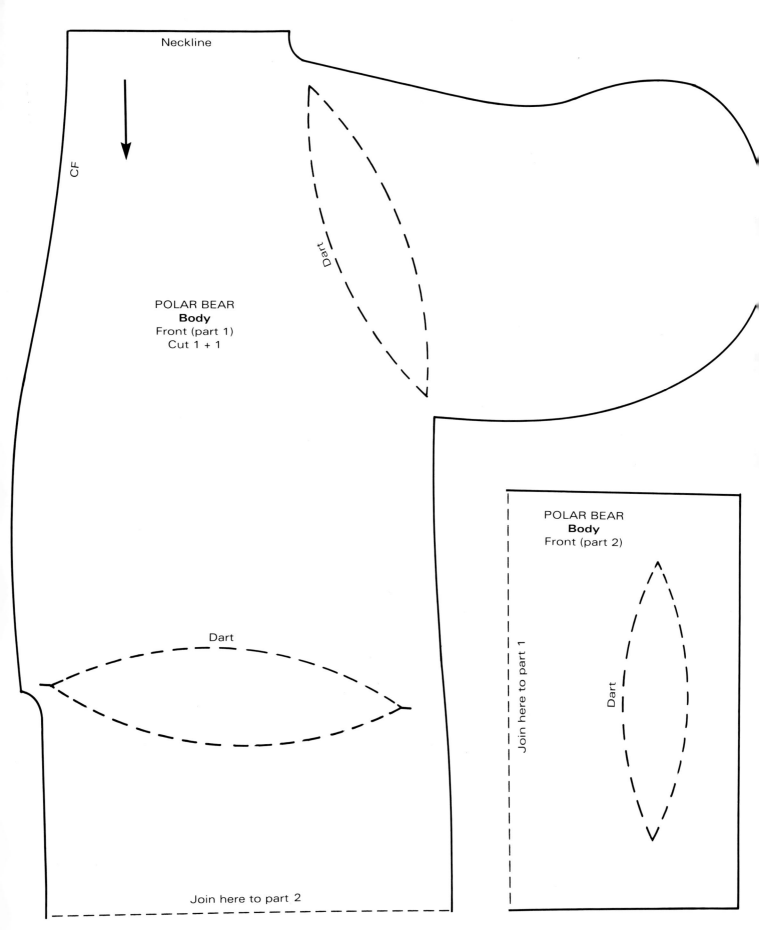

Neckline

CF

POLAR BEAR
Body
Front (part 1)
Cut 1 + 1

Dart

Dart

Join here to part 2

POLAR BEAR
Body
Front (part 2)

Join here to part 1

Dart

30

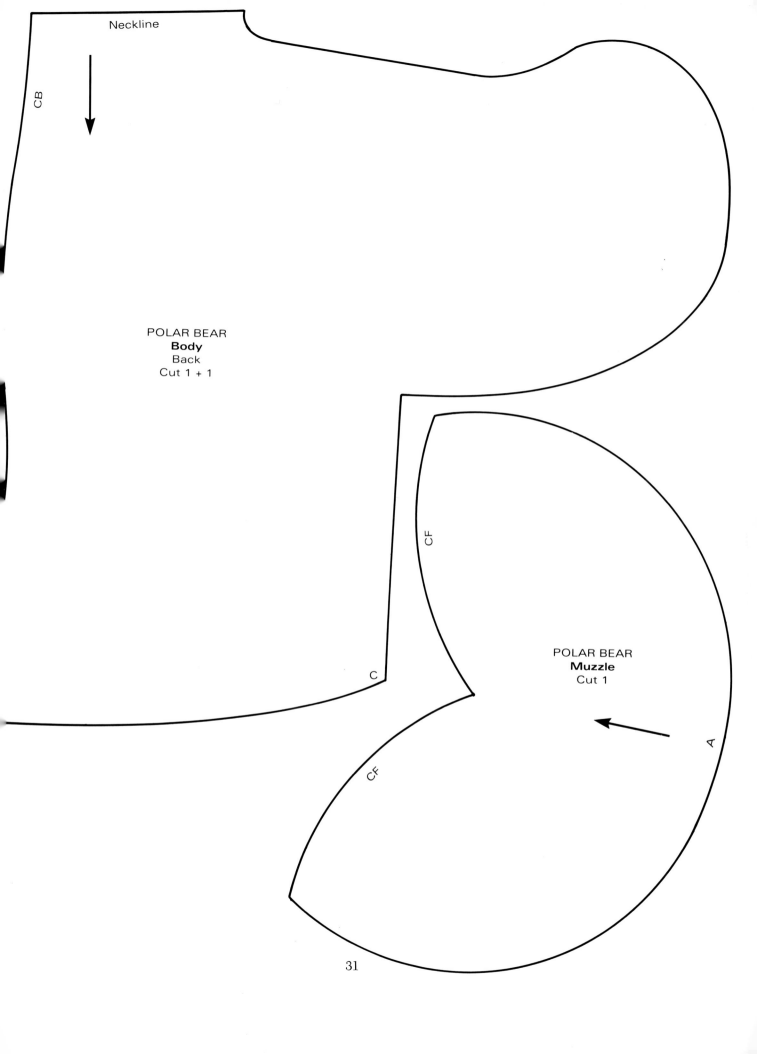

Neckline

CB

POLAR BEAR
Body
Back
Cut 1 + 1

CF

C

POLAR BEAR
Muzzle
Cut 1

CF

A

31

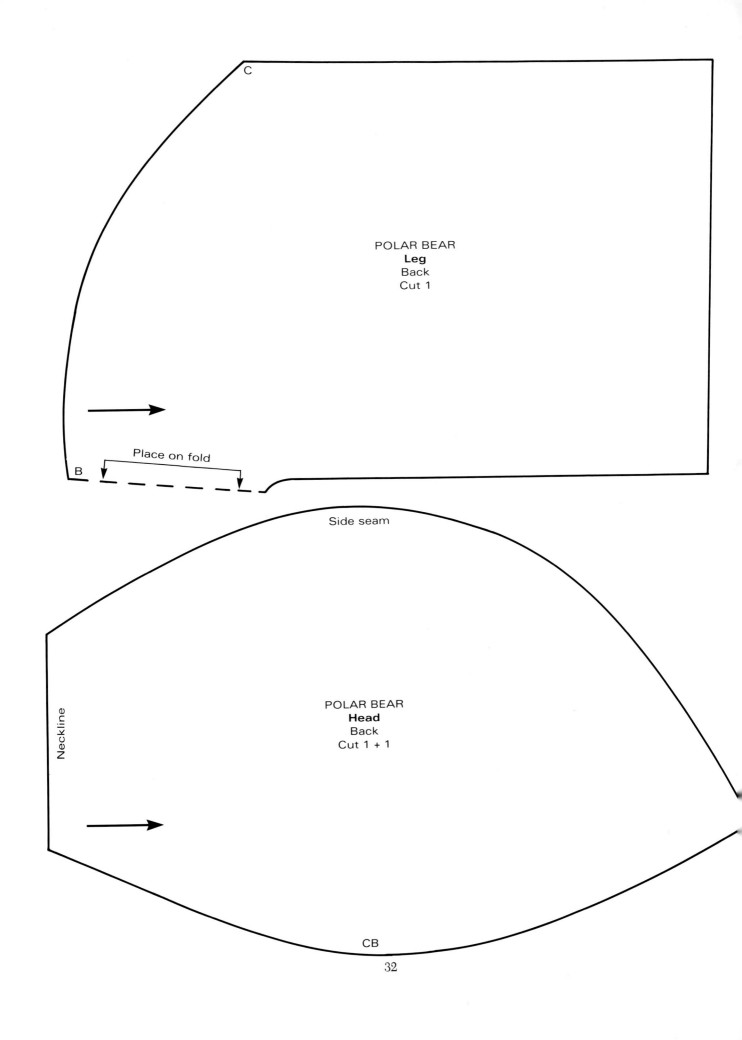

C

POLAR BEAR
Leg
Back
Cut 1

Place on fold

B

Side seam

Neckline

POLAR BEAR
Head
Back
Cut 1 + 1

CB

32

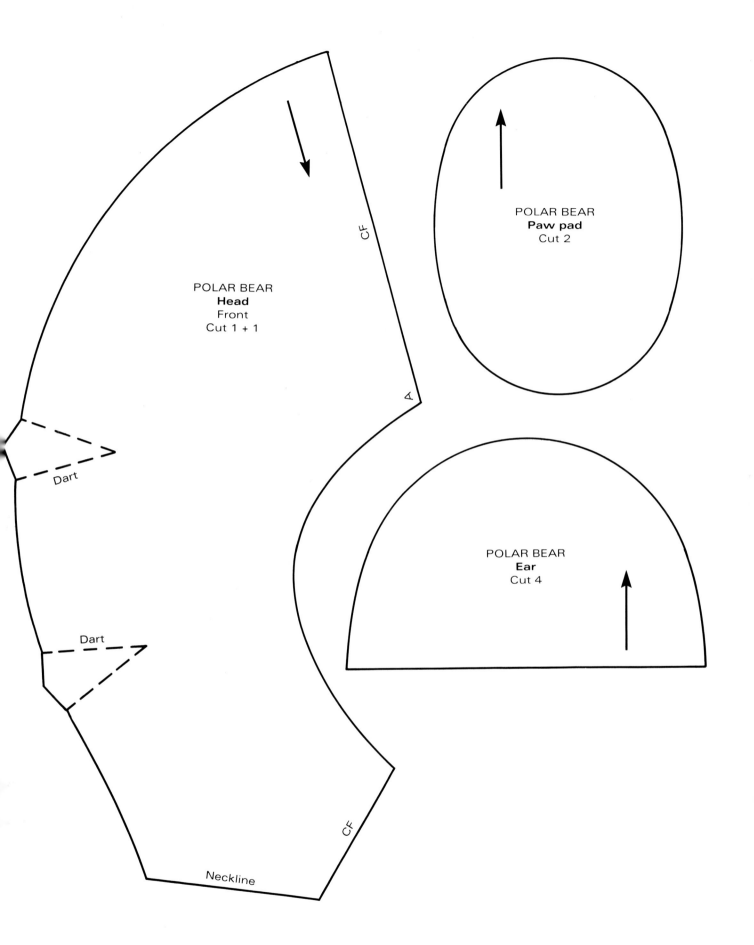

POLAR BEAR
Paw pad
Cut 2

POLAR BEAR
Head
Front
Cut 1 + 1

CF

A

Dart

Dart

Neckline

CF

POLAR BEAR
Ear
Cut 4

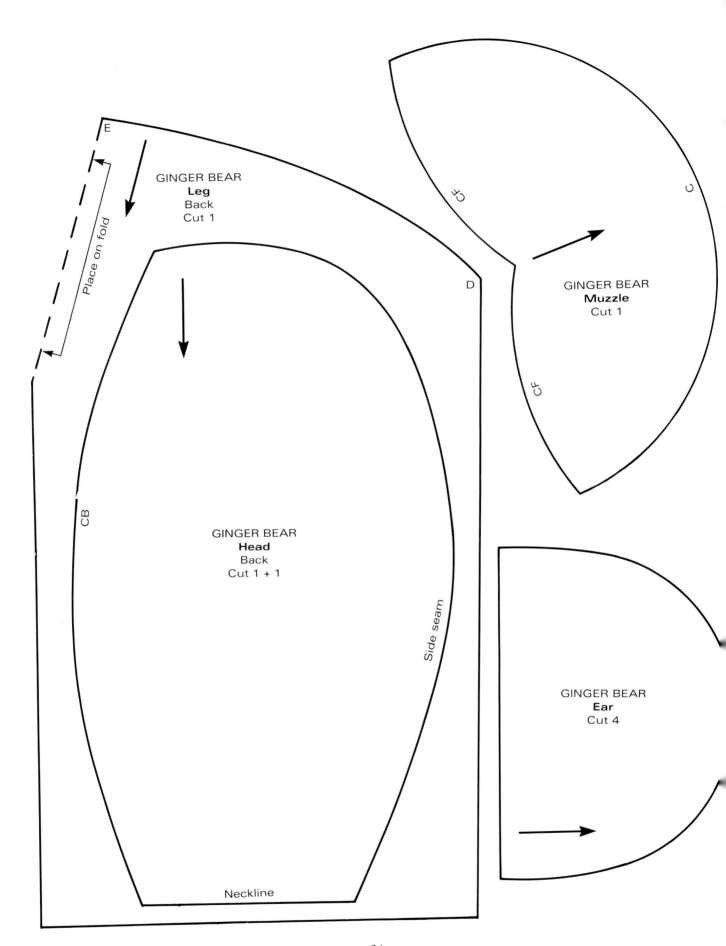

E

GINGER BEAR
Leg
Back
Cut 1

Place on fold

CB

GINGER BEAR
Head
Back
Cut 1 + 1

Side seam

Neckline

D

CF

CF

C

GINGER BEAR
Muzzle
Cut 1

GINGER BEAR
Ear
Cut 4

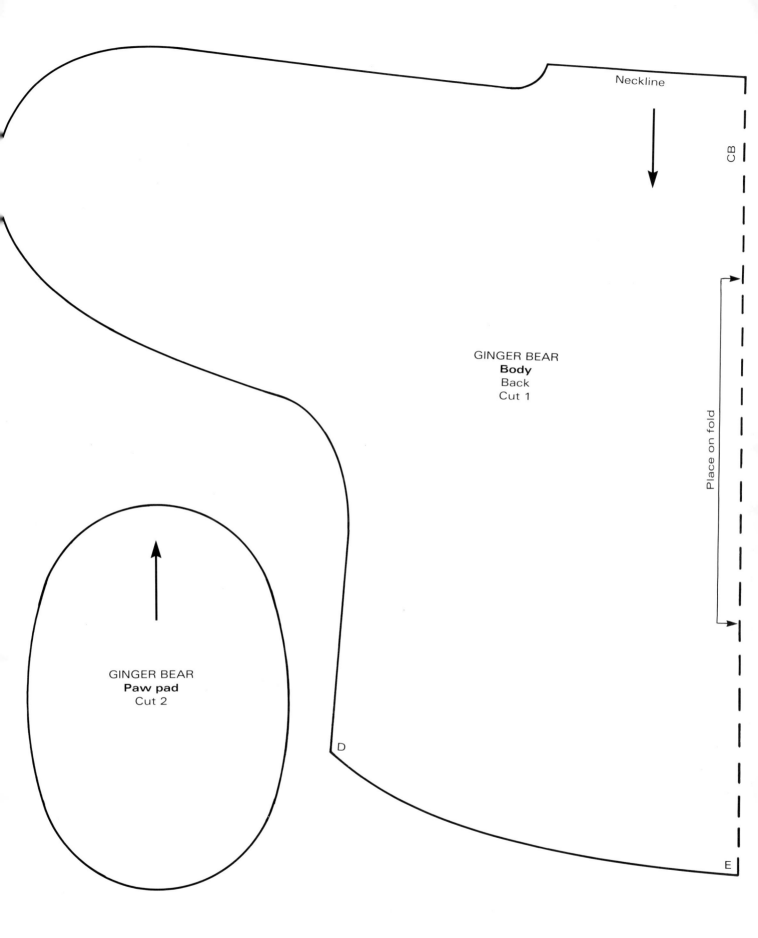

Neckline

CB

GINGER BEAR
Body
Back
Cut 1

Place on fold

GINGER BEAR
Paw pad
Cut 2

D

E

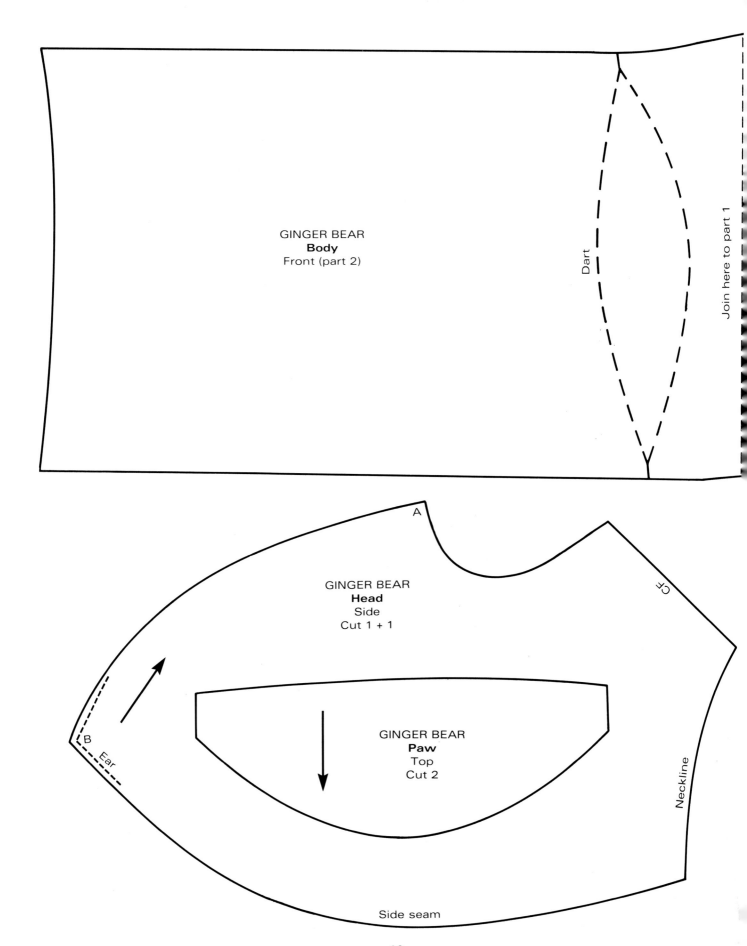

GINGER BEAR
Body
Front (part 2)

Dart

Join here to part 1

A

GINGER BEAR
Head
Side
Cut 1 + 1

CF

B

Ear

GINGER BEAR
Paw
Top
Cut 2

Neckline

Side seam

36

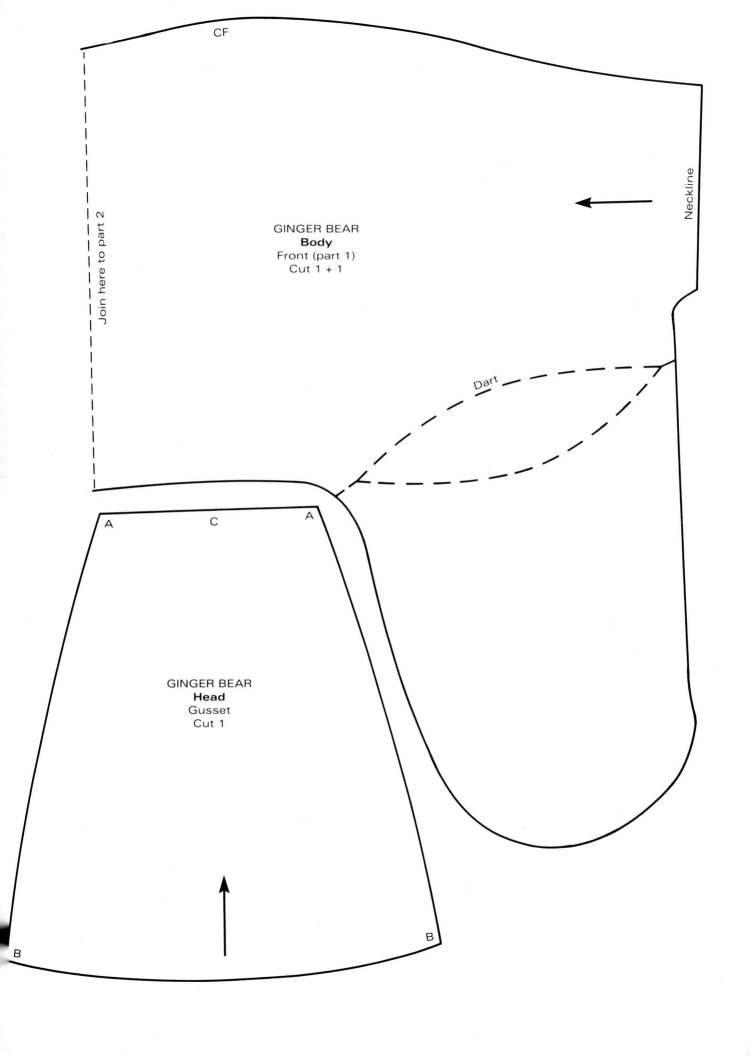

CF

Neckline

Join here to part 2

GINGER BEAR
Body
Front (part 1)
Cut 1 + 1

Dart

A   C   A

GINGER BEAR
Head
Gusset
Cut 1

B

B

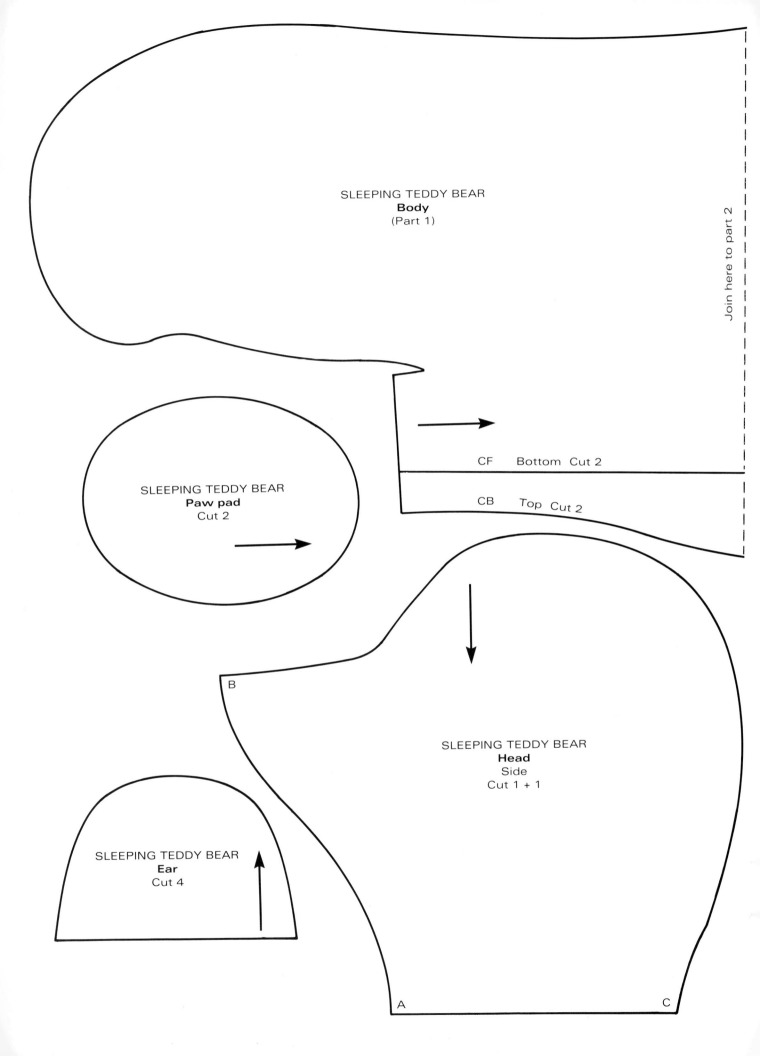

SLEEPING TEDDY BEAR
Body
(Part 1)

Join here to part 2

SLEEPING TEDDY BEAR
Paw pad
Cut 2

CF   Bottom Cut 2

CB   Top Cut 2

B

SLEEPING TEDDY BEAR
Head
Side
Cut 1 + 1

SLEEPING TEDDY BEAR
Ear
Cut 4

A   C

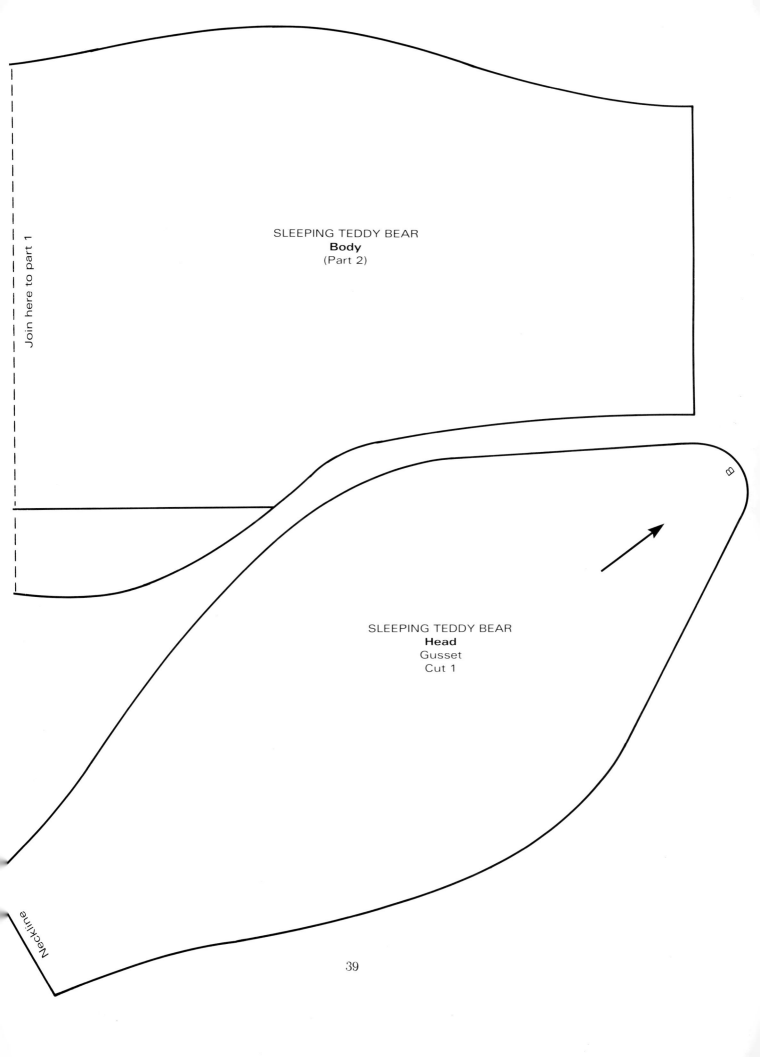

Join here to part 1

SLEEPING TEDDY BEAR
Body
(Part 2)

SLEEPING TEDDY BEAR
Head
Gusset
Cut 1

B

Neckline

39

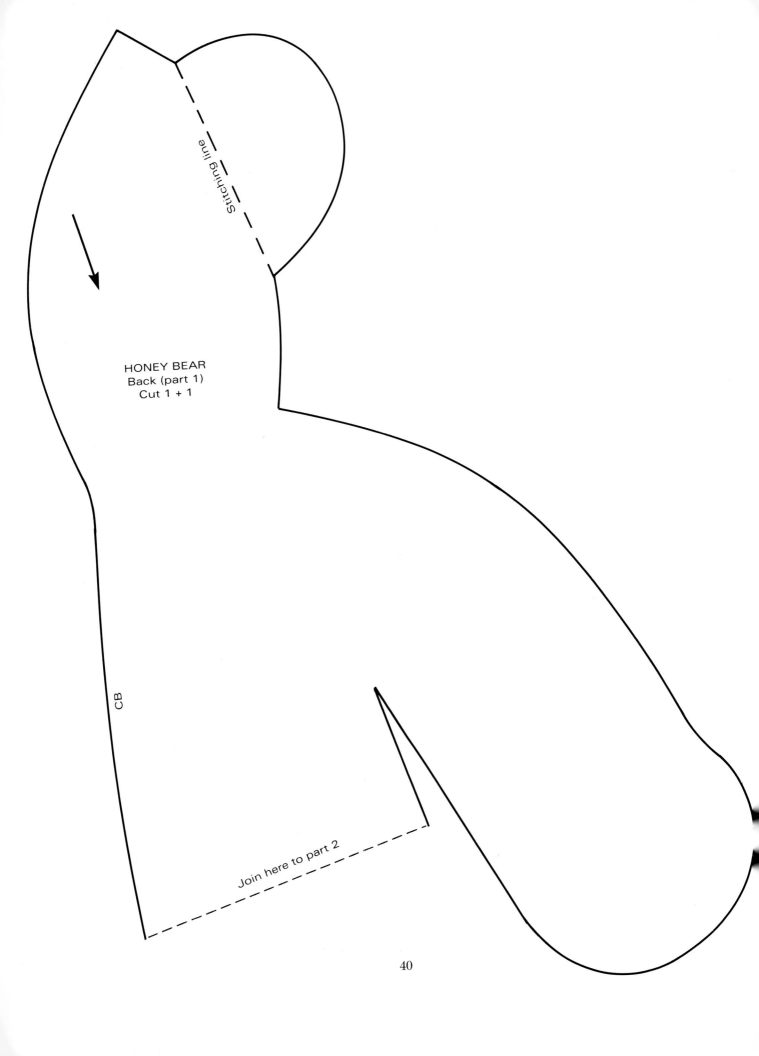

Stitching line

HONEY BEAR
Back (part 1)
Cut 1 + 1

CB

Join here to part 2

40

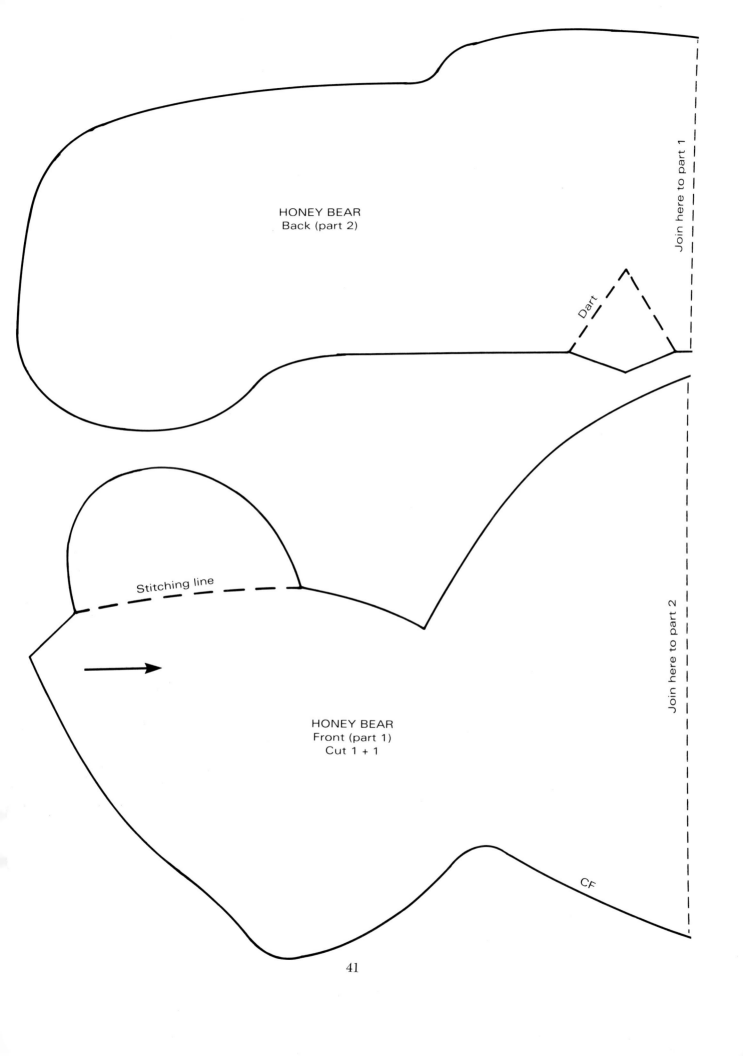

HONEY BEAR
Back (part 2)

Dart

Join here to part 1

Stitching line

Join here to part 2

HONEY BEAR
Front (part 1)
Cut 1 + 1

CF

41

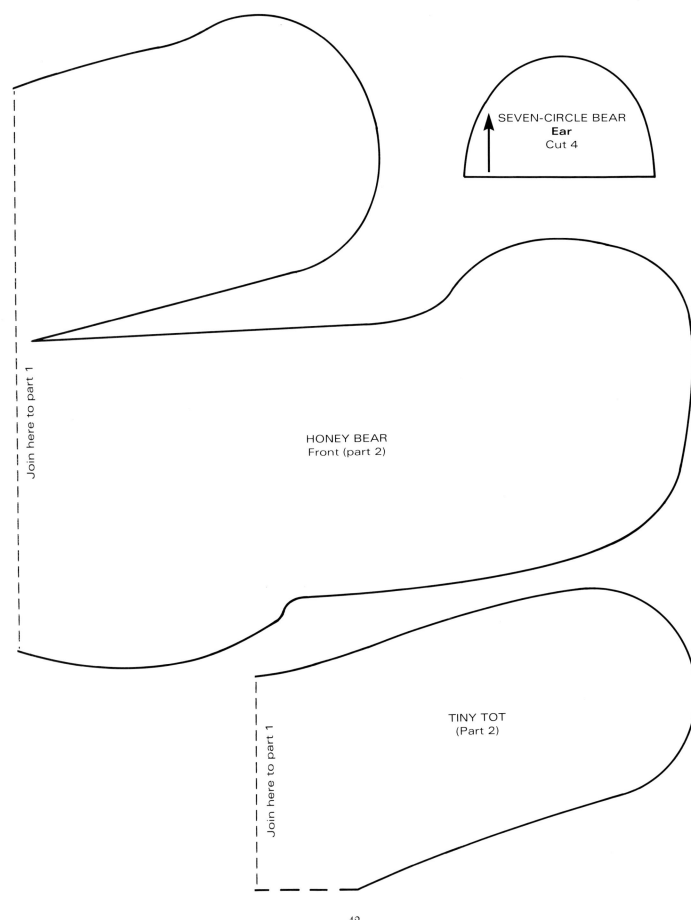

SEVEN-CIRCLE BEAR
Ear
Cut 4

Join here to part 1

HONEY BEAR
Front (part 2)

Join here to part 1

TINY TOT
(Part 2)

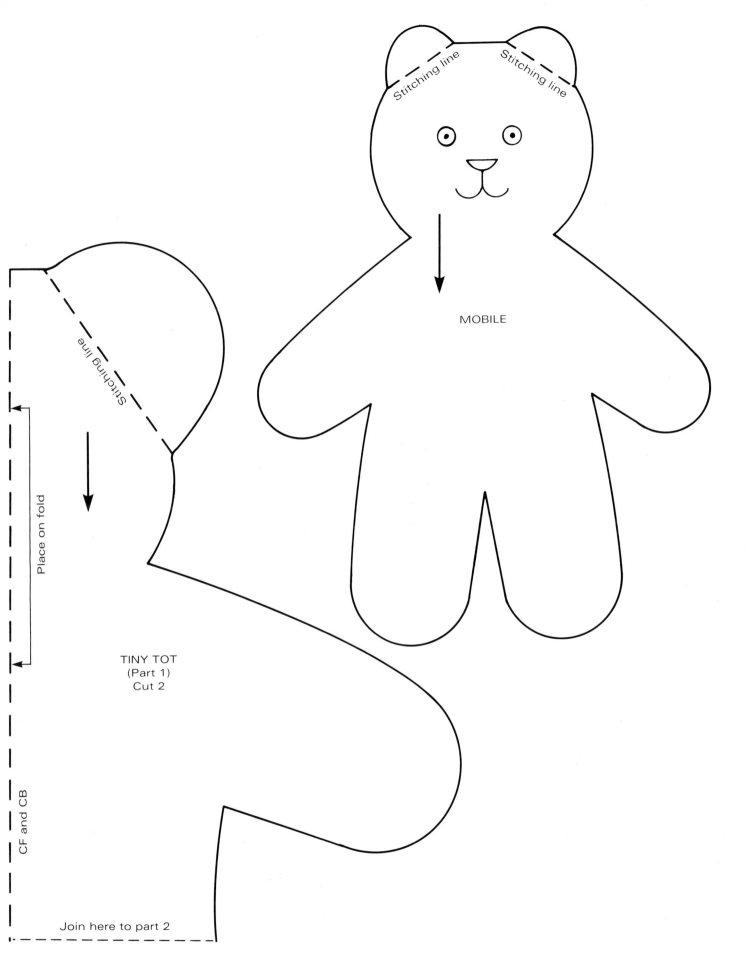

Stitching line

Stitching line

MOBILE

Stitching line

Place on fold

CF and CB

TINY TOT
(Part 1)
Cut 2

Join here to part 2

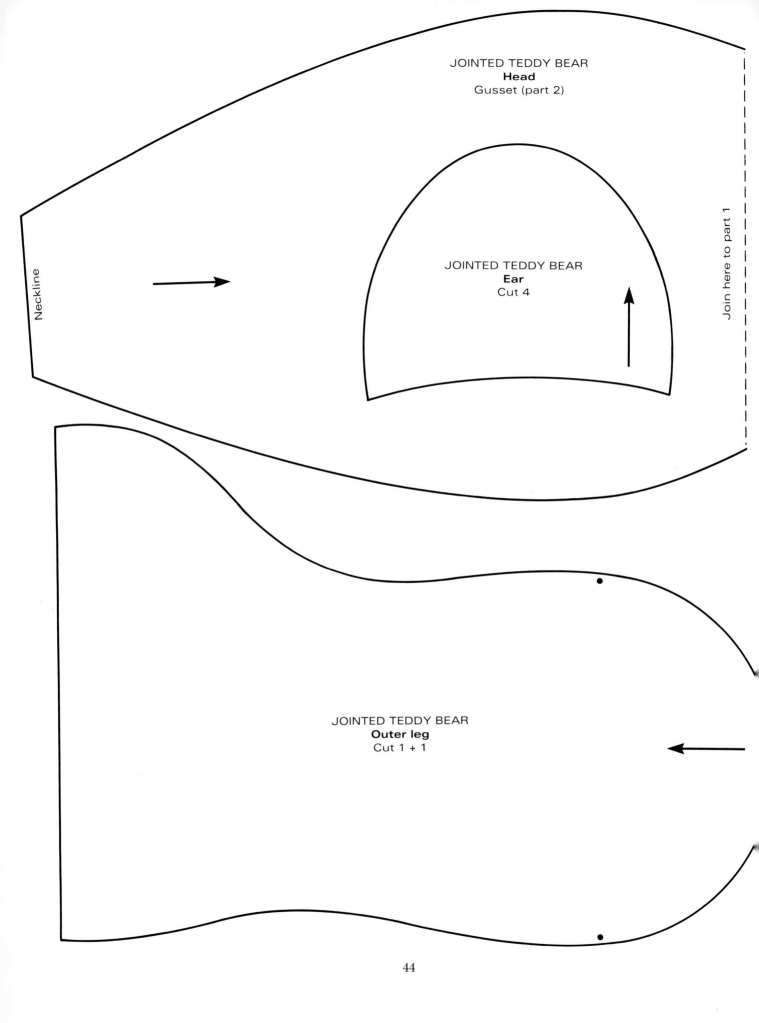

JOINTED TEDDY BEAR
Head
Gusset (part 2)

Neckline

Join here to part 1

JOINTED TEDDY BEAR
Ear
Cut 4

JOINTED TEDDY BEAR
Outer leg
Cut 1 + 1

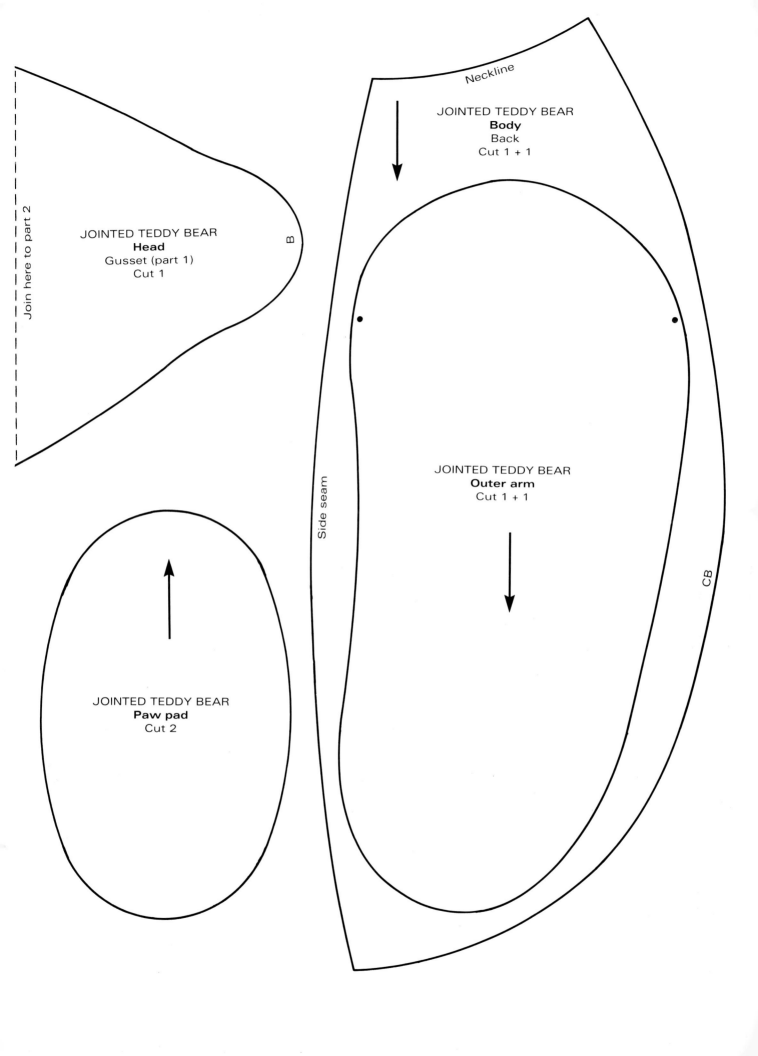

JOINTED TEDDY BEAR
Head
Gusset (part 1)
Cut 1

Join here to part 2

B

JOINTED TEDDY BEAR
Paw pad
Cut 2

Neckline

JOINTED TEDDY BEAR
Body
Back
Cut 1 + 1

Side seam

JOINTED TEDDY BEAR
Outer arm
Cut 1 + 1

CB

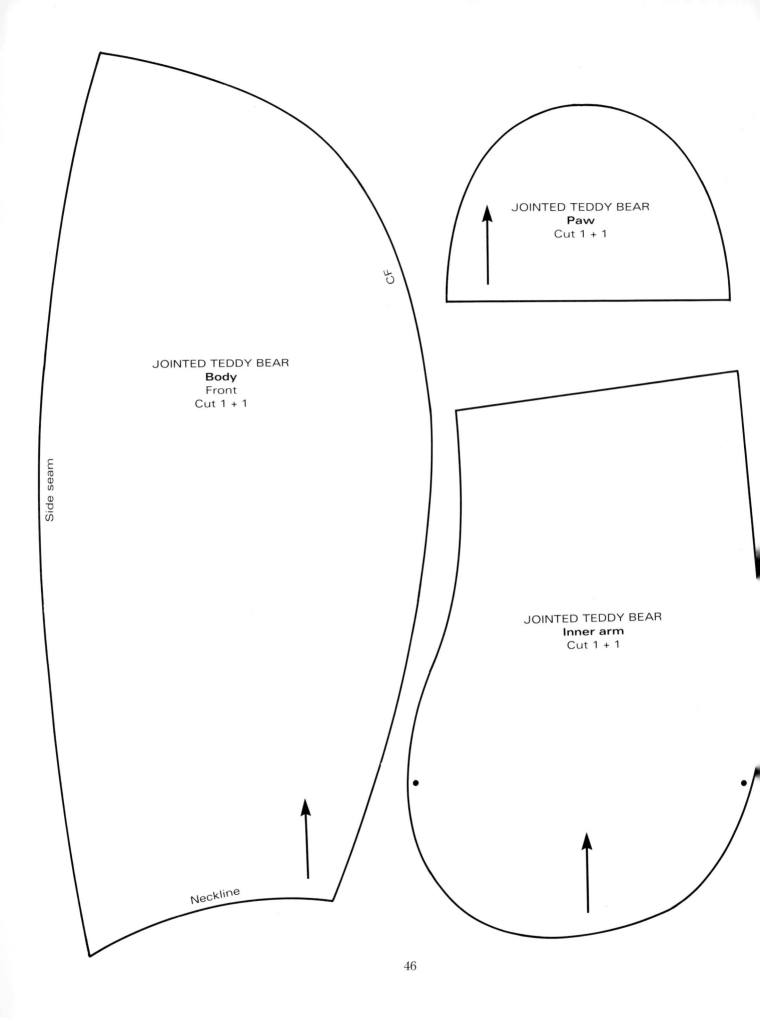

JOINTED TEDDY BEAR
Paw
Cut 1 + 1

JOINTED TEDDY BEAR
Body
Front
Cut 1 + 1

CF

Side seam

Neckline

JOINTED TEDDY BEAR
Inner arm
Cut 1 + 1

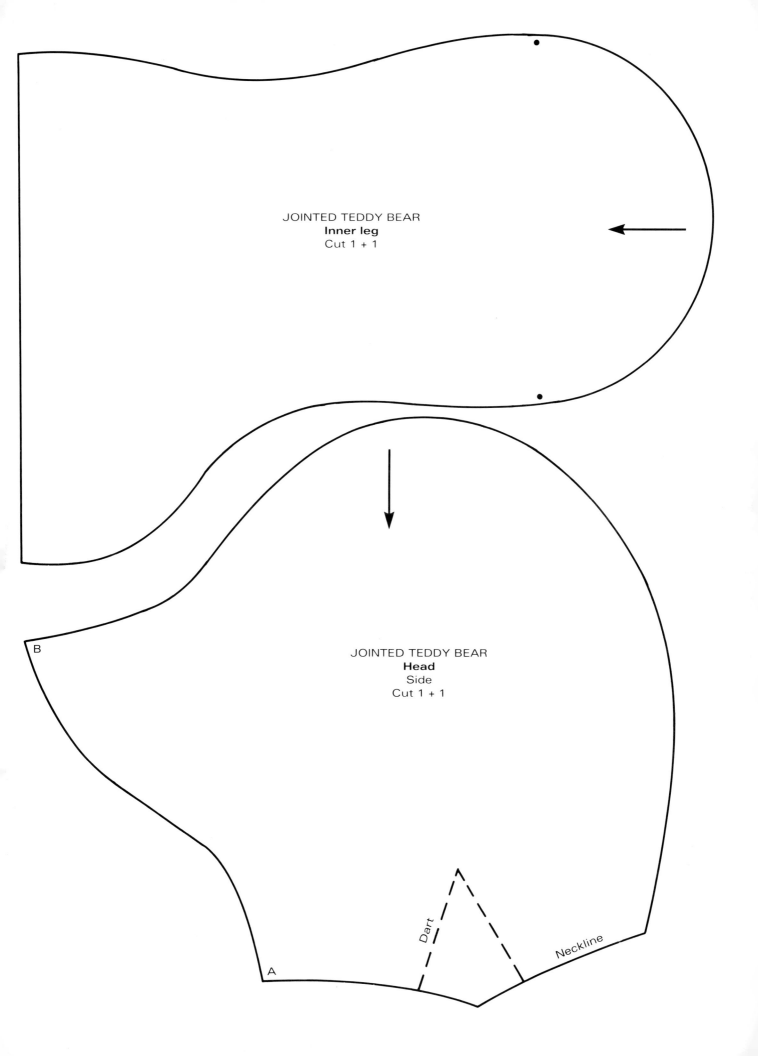

JOINTED TEDDY BEAR
Inner leg
Cut 1 + 1

JOINTED TEDDY BEAR
Head
Side
Cut 1 + 1

B

A

Dart

Neckline

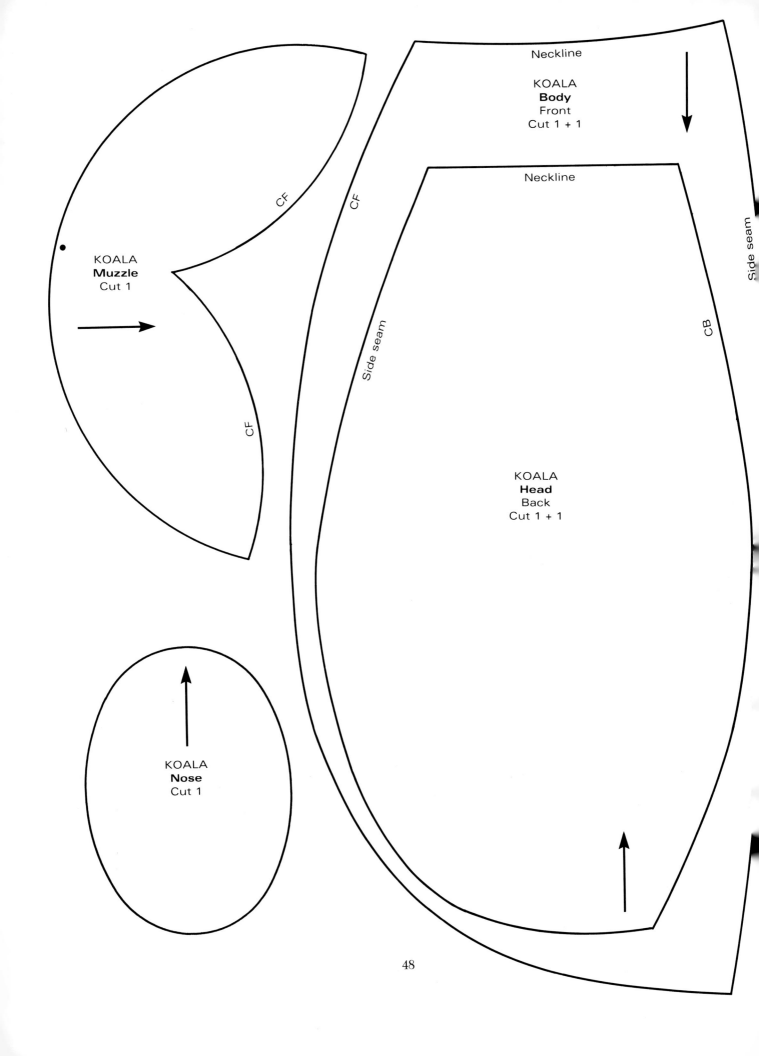

KOALA
Body
Front
Cut 1 + 1

Neckline

Side seam

CF

CF

CF

KOALA
Muzzle
Cut 1

Neckline

Side seam

CB

KOALA
Head
Back
Cut 1 + 1

KOALA
Nose
Cut 1

Neckline

48

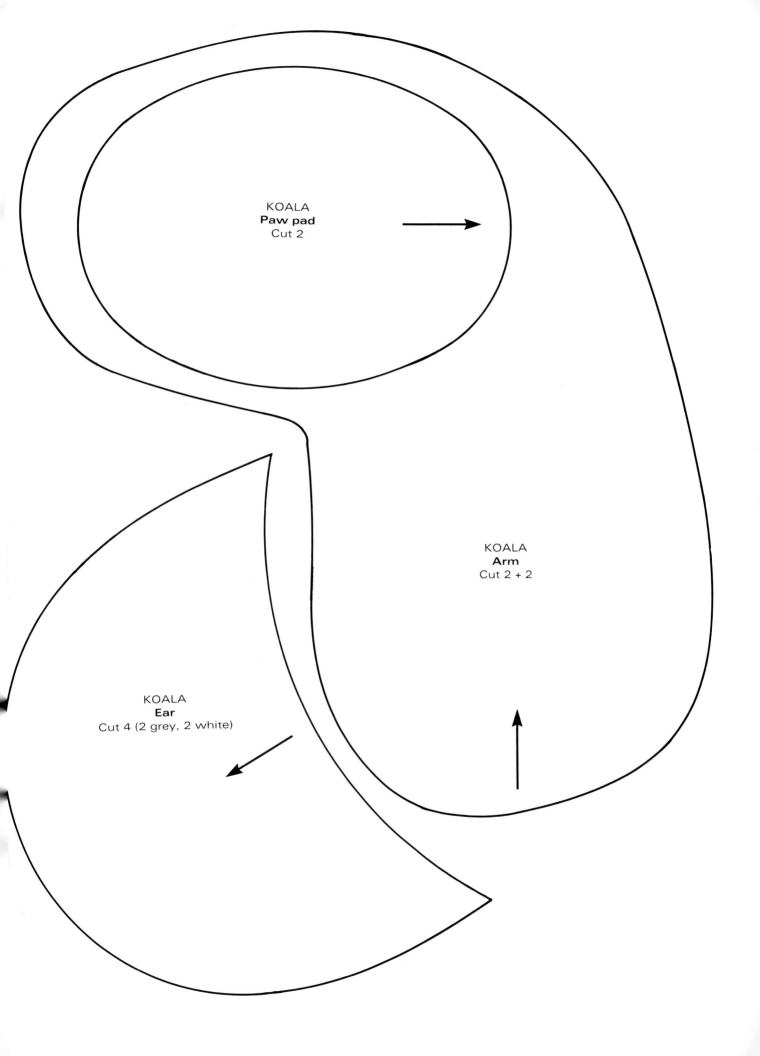

KOALA
Paw pad
Cut 2

KOALA
Arm
Cut 2 + 2

KOALA
Ear
Cut 4 (2 grey, 2 white)

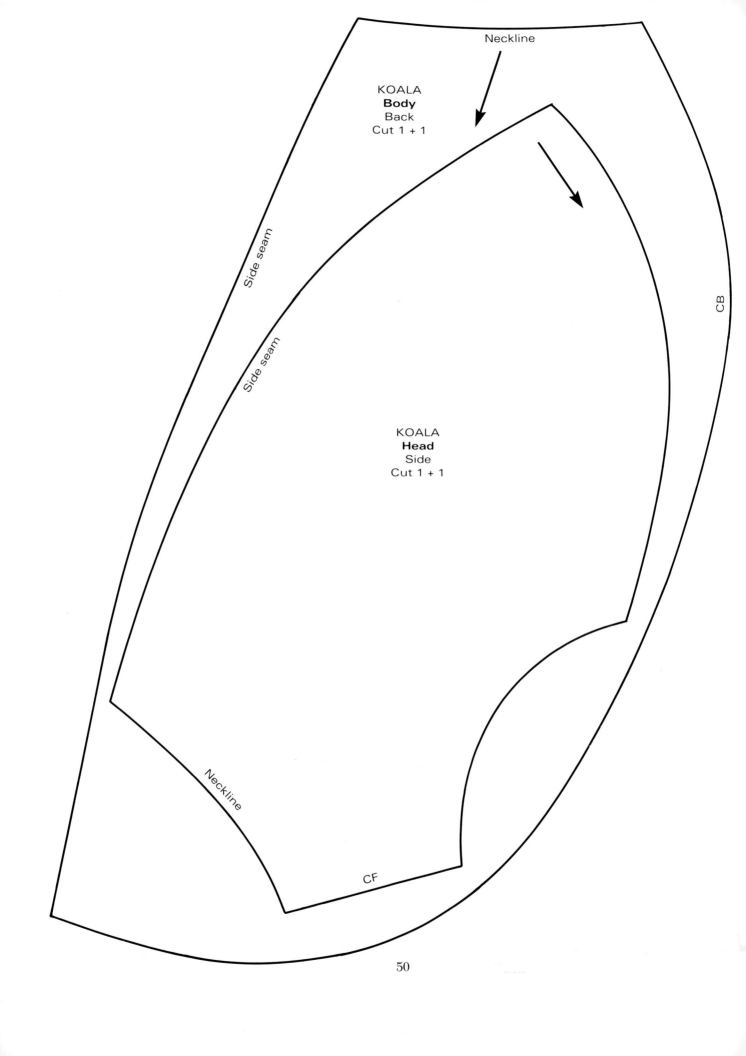

Neckline

KOALA
Body
Back
Cut 1 + 1

Side seam

Side seam

CB

KOALA
Head
Side
Cut 1 + 1

Neckline

CF

50

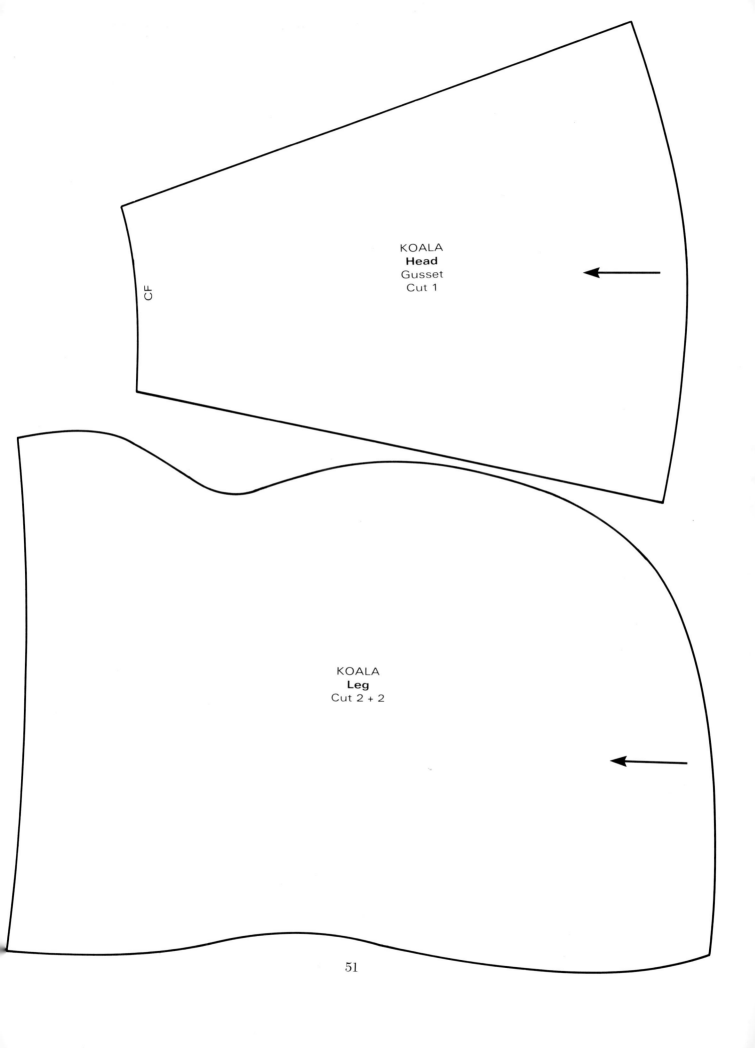

KOALA
Head
Gusset
Cut 1

CF

KOALA
Leg
Cut 2 + 2

51

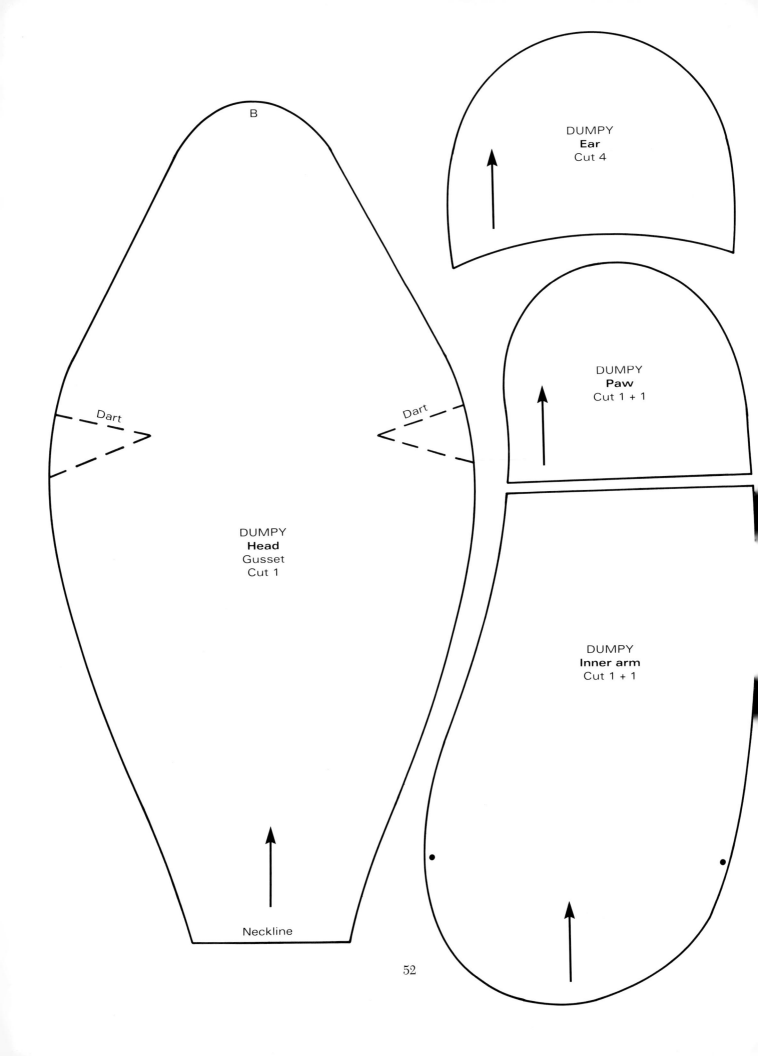

B

Dart

Dart

DUMPY
Head
Gusset
Cut 1

Neckline

DUMPY
Ear
Cut 4

DUMPY
Paw
Cut 1 + 1

DUMPY
Inner arm
Cut 1 + 1

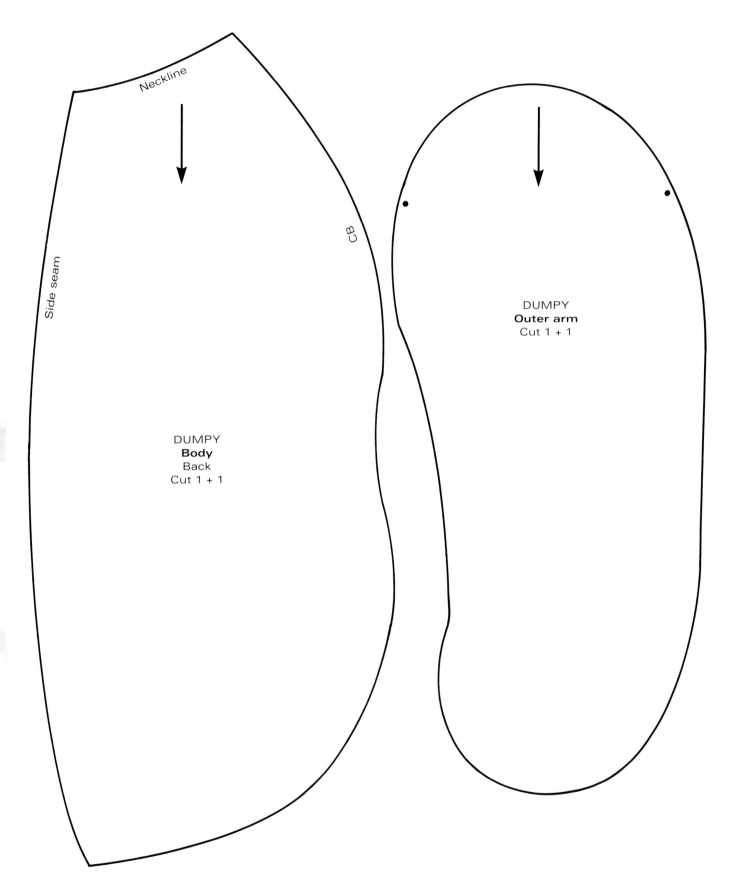

Neckline

Side seam

CB

DUMPY
Body
Back
Cut 1 + 1

DUMPY
Outer arm
Cut 1 + 1

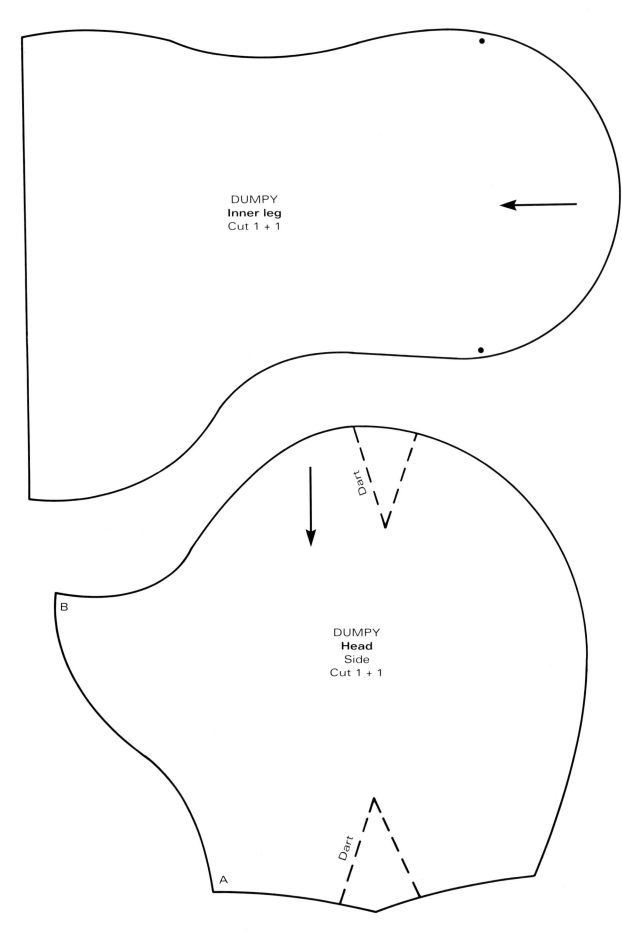

DUMPY
Inner leg
Cut 1 + 1

DUMPY
Head
Side
Cut 1 + 1

Dart

Dart

B

A

54

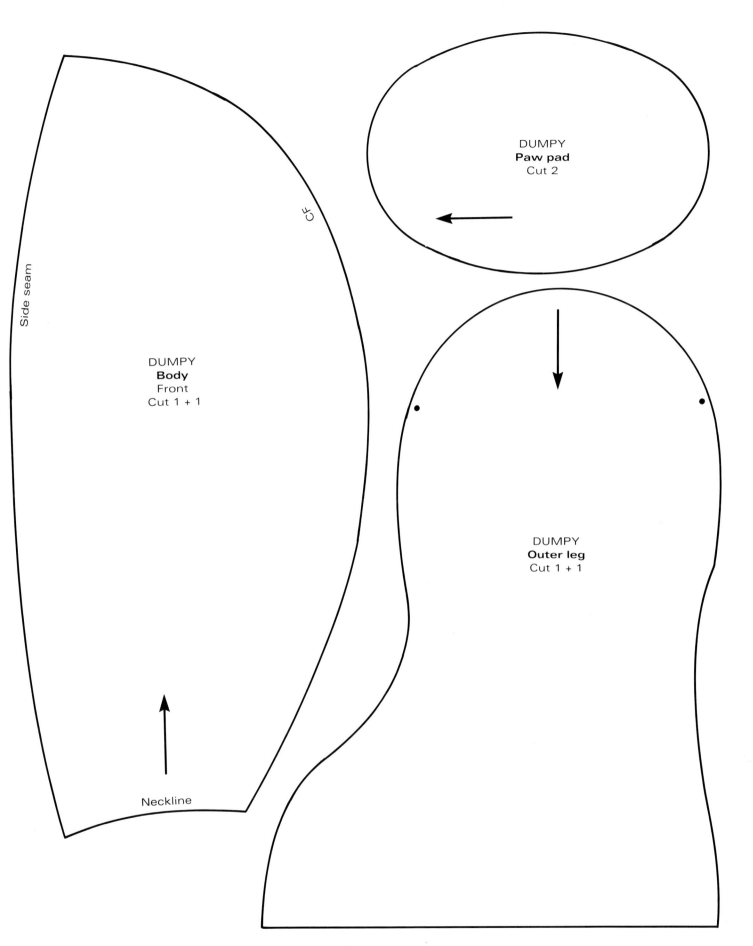

DUMPY
Paw pad
Cut 2

Side seam

CF

DUMPY
Body
Front
Cut 1 + 1

DUMPY
Outer leg
Cut 1 + 1

Neckline

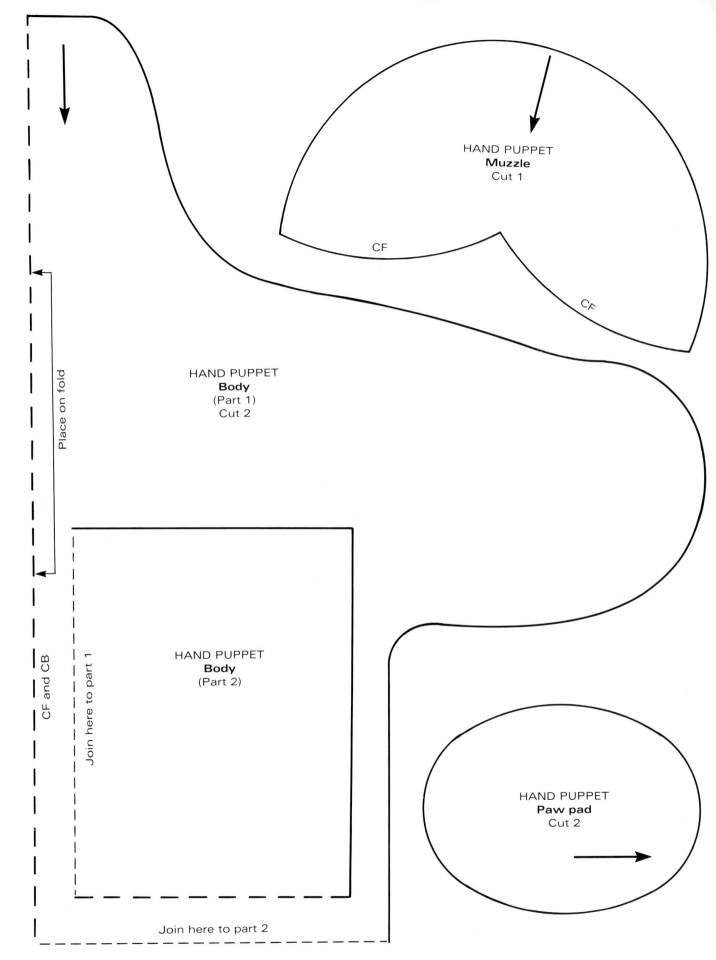

HAND PUPPET
Muzzle
Cut 1

CF

CF

Place on fold

HAND PUPPET
Body
(Part 1)
Cut 2

CF and CB

Join here to part 1

HAND PUPPET
Body
(Part 2)

HAND PUPPET
Paw pad
Cut 2

Join here to part 2

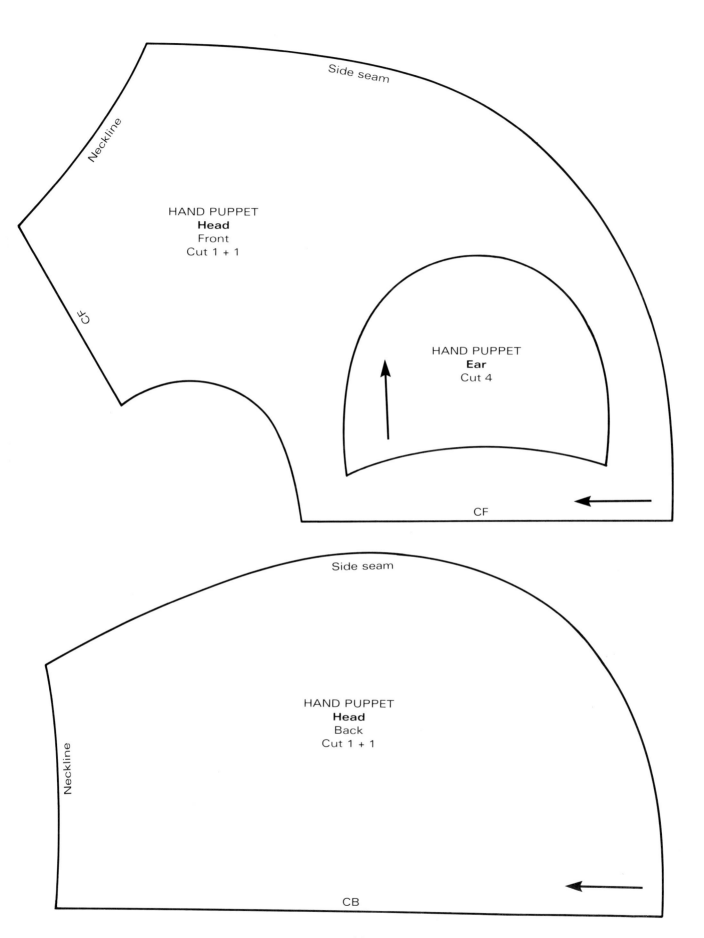

Side seam

Neckline

HAND PUPPET
Head
Front
Cut 1 + 1

CF

HAND PUPPET
Ear
Cut 4

CF

Side seam

Neckline

HAND PUPPET
Head
Back
Cut 1 + 1

CB

57

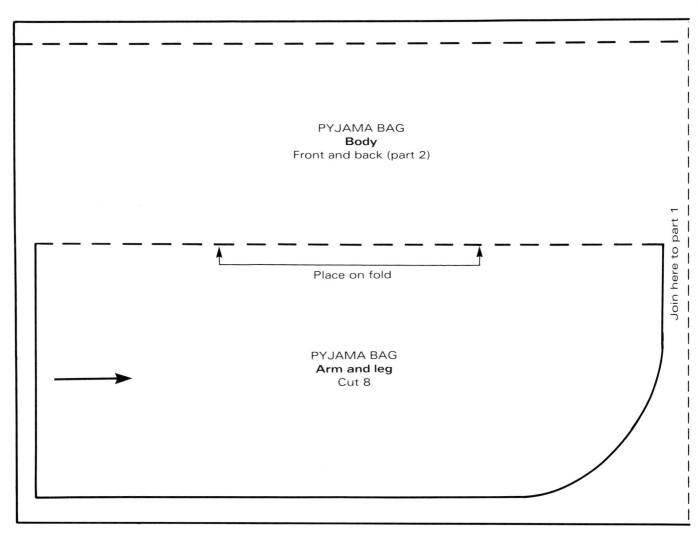

PYJAMA BAG
Body
Front and back (part 2)

Join here to part 1

Place on fold

PYJAMA BAG
Arm and leg
Cut 8

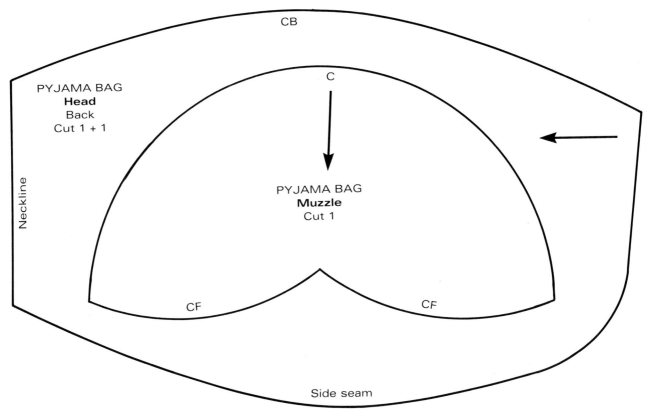

CB

C

PYJAMA BAG
Head
Back
Cut 1 + 1

Neckline

PYJAMA BAG
Muzzle
Cut 1

CF

CF

Side seam

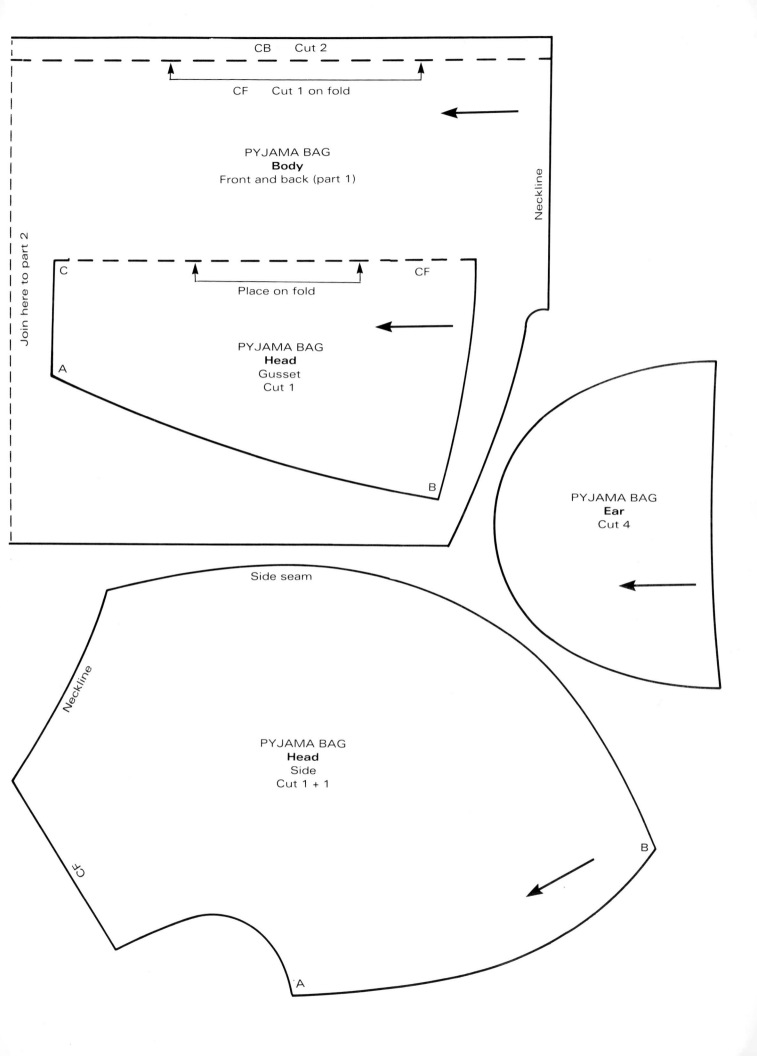

CB   Cut 2

CF   Cut 1 on fold

PYJAMA BAG
Body
Front and back (part 1)

Neckline

Join here to part 2

C

CF

Place on fold

A

PYJAMA BAG
Head
Gusset
Cut 1

B

PYJAMA BAG
Ear
Cut 4

Side seam

Neckline

B

PYJAMA BAG
Head
Side
Cut 1 + 1

CF

A

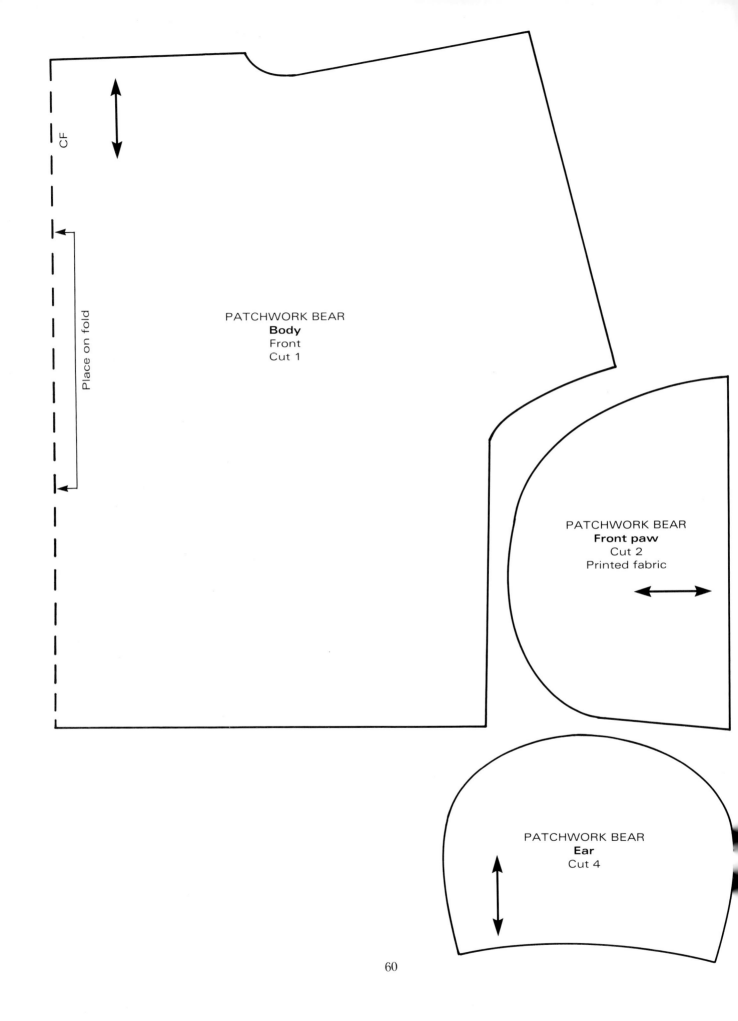

CF

Place on fold

PATCHWORK BEAR
Body
Front
Cut 1

PATCHWORK BEAR
Front paw
Cut 2
Printed fabric

PATCHWORK BEAR
Ear
Cut 4

60

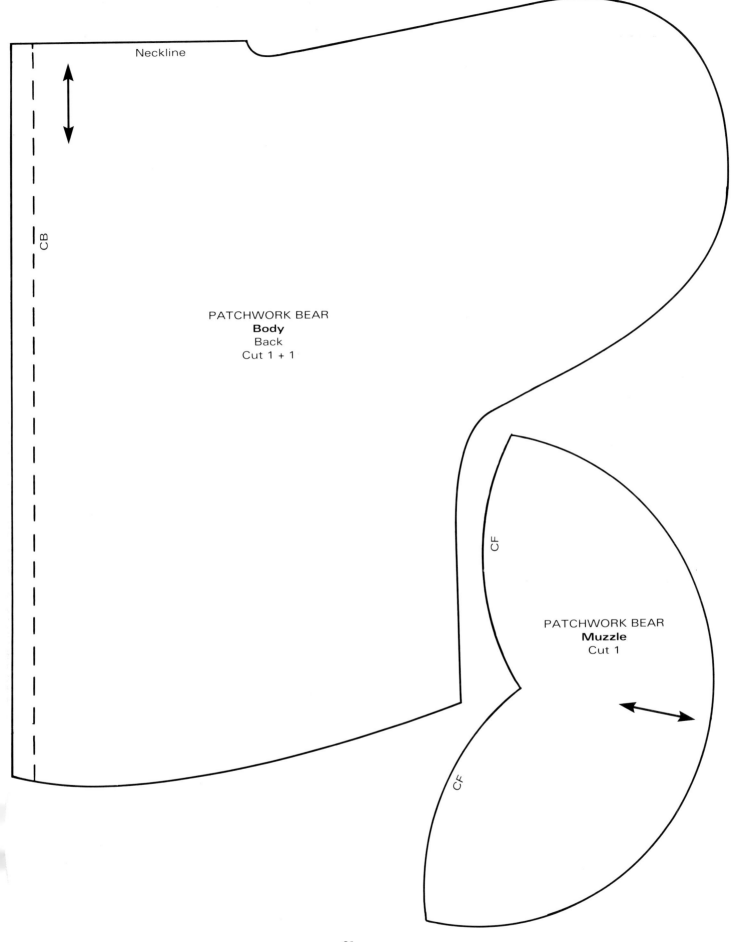

Neckline

CB

PATCHWORK BEAR
Body
Back
Cut 1 + 1

CF

PATCHWORK BEAR
Muzzle
Cut 1

CF

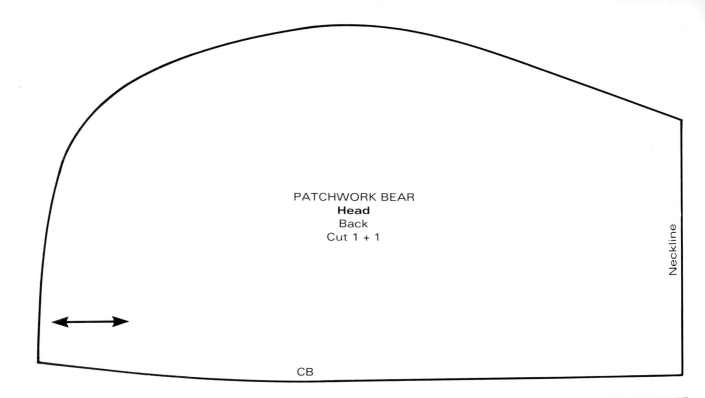

PATCHWORK BEAR
Head
Back
Cut 1 + 1

Neckline

CB

CF

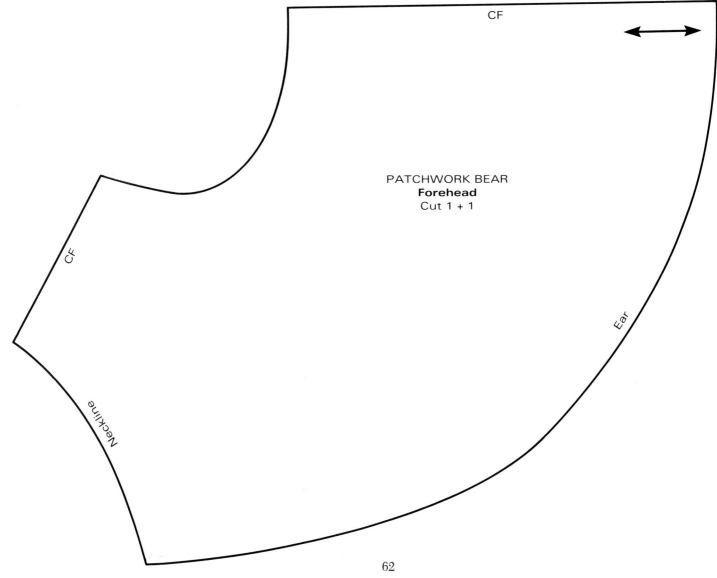

PATCHWORK BEAR
Forehead
Cut 1 + 1

CF

Ear

Neckline

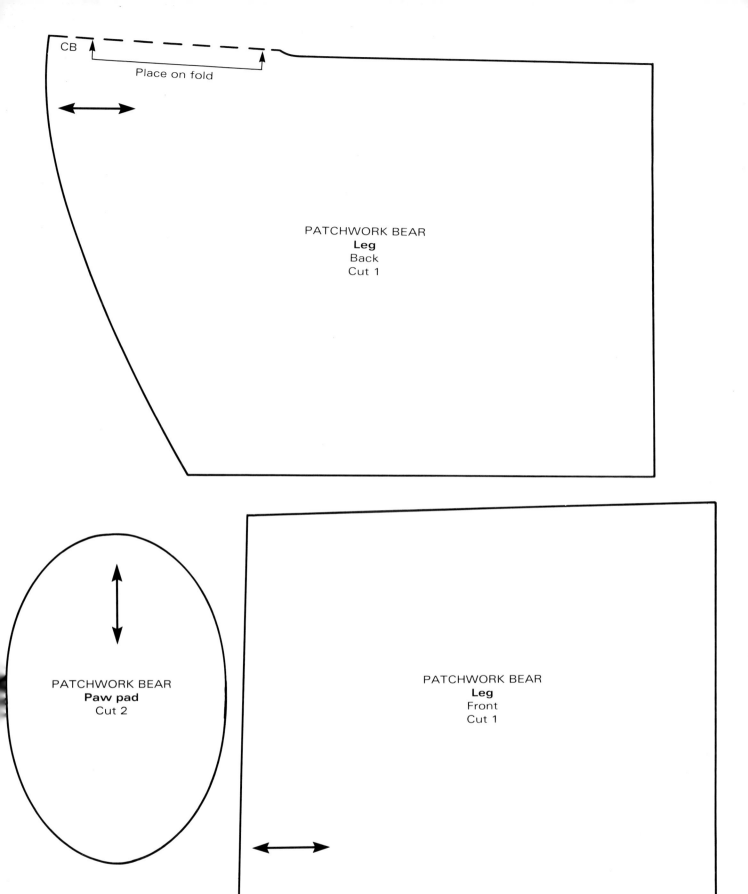

CB

Place on fold

PATCHWORK BEAR
Leg
Back
Cut 1

PATCHWORK BEAR
Paw pad
Cut 2

PATCHWORK BEAR
Leg
Front
Cut 1

Place on fold

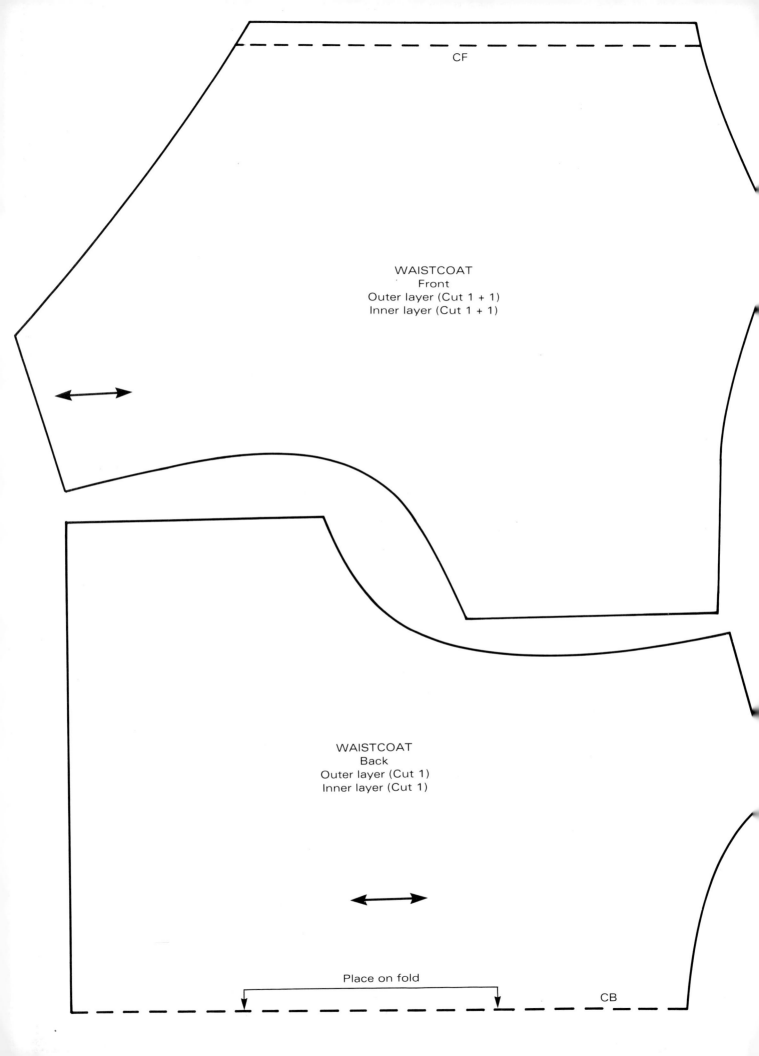

WAISTCOAT
Front
Outer layer (Cut 1 + 1)
Inner layer (Cut 1 + 1)

CF

WAISTCOAT
Back
Outer layer (Cut 1)
Inner layer (Cut 1)

Place on fold

CB